Gathered Words

An Anthology of Writing from The Writers Community

Edited by Lynne Golodner

Scotia Road Books

Contents

Foreword

Lynne Golodner

I first started teaching writing in my 20s, as an MFA student at Goddard College. It was a "terminal teaching degree," one where we pursued our love of writing (for me, it was poetry back then), and simultaneously learned how to teach creative writing in the real world. At first, I taught children mostly, and later in my 20s, MFA in hand, I poured my entrepreneurial zeal into creating summer writing camps for children.

My 20s were a long time ago, and I've taught ever since—at universities, as adjunct faculty and a guest lecturer, in synagogues and community centers, and when I pivoted my career to lessen the amount of marketing and public relations work I was doing, and ramp up my own writing, I got back to teaching writing with renewed energy. I began teaching online classes for WritingWorkshops.com, and met a crop of amazing aspiring writers, who kept wanting to work together. And, I know well the power of a supportive, encouraging community of writers to hold each other accountable. From that desire, The Writers Community was born.

I started The Writers Community in 2021, and it has evolved each year since. (Learn all about it at https://lynnegolodner.com/write-with-lynn

e/) There is so much talent among the writers who have come through this program, that I wanted to celebrate their voices by producing this anthology.

In this book, you'll find beautiful stories of love, loss, family, adventure, self-discovery, redemption, and second chances. The women in this collection (there are men in TWC as well, just not in this anthology) offer poetry, flash, fiction, and creative nonfiction from the United States, Canada and Scotland. They are brave and strong, vulnerable and courageous.

As every good writer should be.

While focusing on the details of daily life, the details of mundane, ordinary life, the writers in this collection are speaking to our deepest questions: Who am I? Why am I here? What is the purpose of human life? Am I making a difference? Do I matter?

And their answers are poetically resonant, deeply satisfying, simply brilliant.

In this collection, I see resilience. Power in the form of community. A reclaiming of voice and of vision at whatever point in life we feel the urge to stand up and say, "This is me!"

I am honored to be trusted with these beautiful voices, and to share them with readers who want to discover new voices with eye-opening revelations and perspectives about the human condition. These writers know how to live and to celebrate the beauty that is all around us. I only hope that their voices provide hope for a resilient, powerful future for us all.

Fiction

Fractured Time

ALYSSA MUSSO

A giggle drifts in the wind as her chestnut hair flows around her. She had left her hat inside.

"Maddie! Wait up!"

But Maddie continues to run, laughing. She spins and twirls, her coat flapping. It is below freezing outside, but she doesn't mind. One of her pink mittens drops into the snow.

"You dropped your mitten!"

Reaching for it, a shriek pierces the air. She disappears into a dark hole.

"Maddie!"

***

"Marcie! Marcie, can you hear me? Wake up! Marceline!"

A firm hand on her shoulder rips Marcie from the past. Her heart pounds in her ears; she shivers, her skin coated in a cold sweat. Pale moonlight casts shadows of worry on Wes's face, but Marcie's muscles soften, and her breathing slows at the sight of her husband. She unclenches her fists, releasing the bedsheets from her clammy palms, and inhales as Wes pushes a plastered strand of brown hair from her cheek.

She stares into his hazel eyes. The golden flecks in his irises glimmer in the low light. She swallows without saying a word. Wes presses his lips into a thin line. After twelve years of sharing a bed, there is no need for further explanation. He's accustomed to Maddie's name puncturing the night, his wife thrashing beside him as she's thrown back into a memory that has haunted her for decades.

Wes pulls Marcie against his bare chest. She closes her eyes, focusing on his heartbeat. The rhythm starts out as a strong drumming, but quickly subsides into a gentle thumping, shepherding her own heart back to a comfortable place. Within minutes, their hearts beat in unison. Marcie falls asleep enveloped by her husband's warmth rather than encased by the frigid hold of her past.

***

The clattering of dishes awakens Marcie the next morning. She groans and blinks, shocked at the numbers on the clock: 9:27.

She throws the comforter aside and pulls a sweatshirt over her head. Brushing her long hair in the mirror, Marcie wonders if she and Maddie would still look so much alike, thirty years later. She stares at her blue eyes and tries not to think of the bluish pallor of Maddie's skin when they pulled her from the lake.

Marcie shuffles downstairs and squints against the blinding light reflecting off a fresh layer of snow out the window. . In the kitchen, she watches Wes empty the dishwasher. At the table, six-year-old Brayden sits cross-legged on his chair, a brown crayon in his hand as he concentrates on his newest masterpiece. The scraping of Marcie's slippers on the linoleum breaks the boy's focus, a toothy grin spreading across his face.

"You were a sleepyhead this morning, Mommy!"

She ruffles Brayden's golden hair and plants a kiss on his head.

Thank you, she mouths to Wes, and he smiles.

"We had a boys-only breakfast," Brayden says, his honey-brown eyes shining. Marcie cherishes Brayden's likeness to his father.

"What was for breakfast?" Marcie asks.

"It's a secret!"

Brayden catches Wes's gaze; Wes winks, shrugs, and says, "Boys only."

"I guess I'm on my own then," Marcie says, surveying the evidence on the counter surrounding the stove. A griddle pan, spatters of batter, and rogue chocolate chips dot the white marble.

Brayden returns to his drawing as Marcie grabs a bowl from the cabinet and slides a box of Cheerios out from the corner of the counter. Wes whispers in her ear.

"You know, I could make an exception and make you the secret breakfast."

He kisses her temple, and she smiles. "Thank you, but I'll go with the simple girls-only breakfast today."

On cue, Winnie trots into the kitchen, her paws tapping happily across the floor. She sits at Marcie's side as she pours cereal into the bowl. Marcie pulls milk from the fridge, and Winnie whines impatiently.

Marcie sighs, adding Cheerios toWinnie's bowl and patting her fluffy copper head. The dog's tufted tail swishes back and forth as she gobbles the cereal.

Marcie splashes milk into her own bowl. The calendar on the side of the fridge taunts her. She doesn't need to look to know what tomorrow marks. Setting down the milk, she closes her eyes, focusing on the steady inhale and exhale of her breath. The subtle creep of a migraine permeates the hollows behind her eyes. Marcie grips the edge of the counter, willing the pain to dissipate.

She flinches at the gentle touch of Wes's palm against the small of her back. The heat of his skin burns through her sweatshirt.

"Everything okay?"

She nods and takes a deep breath. "It's just a migraine."

"Take it easy today. I'll keep Brayden entertained," Wes says as he rubs her back.

"I love you," Marcie whispers.

"I love you, too." He squeezes her shoulder and adds, "Take your meds and rest."

Wes leaves her standing at the counter, staring down at her soggy cereal. She plays with the Cheerios, submerging them with her spoon until they pop back up. Sometimes she feels like one of the Cheerios, only she can't always find her way back to the surface.

Marcie shakes her head, trying to rid herself of the heavy thoughts that weigh her down. She reaches for the pill bottle in the cabinet and swallows her medication, hoping it will give her some relief.

She brings her bowl to the kitchen table. Brayden draws a pink crayon across the page. Marcie faces her son.

"Pink, huh? That's a new color for you. Expanding your palette?"

Brayden shrugs. "It's the color of the girl's jacket."

"What girl, sweetie?"

"The girl I see outside sometimes."

"A girl from school?" Marcie asks as she eats her cereal.

"No," Brayden says. "Sometimes I see her outside in the backyard, by the lake." He pauses his coloring and points out the window toward the frozen, snow-covered lake.

Marcie's heart leaps into her throat. She drops her spoon into the bowl. Shifting her gaze to Brayden's drawing, she looks closer. Her heart rate spikes as her eyes land on a little girl with brown hair and a pink jacket in a snowy scene. Suddenly, she feels lightheaded.

"Mommy, are you okay? What'swrong?" Brayden's eyes are wide.

Marcie stands, scuffing her chair against the floor. Wes rushes over.

"Hey, what's going on?"

A throbbing in her forehead jumbles her thoughts as she tries to speak. "I... I need to lie down."

The brightness of the sun becomes overwhelming, and colors swirl in front of her. Wes leads her to the couch. Her vision darkens around the edges as she sinks into the cushions. Wes's voice barely registers as she falls into suspended consciousness.

***

A child's squeal of excitement wafts through the air as snow flurries glimmer against a soft, gray sky. In the distance, a boy chases a blur of pink. His small body gallops through the powdery snow, his feet landing on fragile ground.

"Brayden!"

But the wind howls, and the snow quickly becomes an opaque cloak, hiding another world.

***

Marcie bolts upright, her chest heaving. She jumps from the couch and runs to the door leading to the back yard.

Brayden.

The cold sears her lungs, her breath crystallizing in front of her as she steps outside.

"Brayden!"

Her limbs and chest burn with urgency as she stumbles through the drifts. She can't find her son's small footprints in the blowing snow. Marcie pushes forward, shielding her eyes from the blinding sheet of white as snow freezes to her eyelashes. A gust unsteadies her, but she holds herself upright.

A burst of color breaks through the white. Marcie's heart threatens to shatter in the bitter cold. As she reaches for the small pink object, the wind tugs it free, pulling it further, taunting Marcie in its game of deception. She follows, grabbing at it with numbed fingers, but it disappears in the squall. She trips, falling to her knees. In a whirl of white, she can only see a glimpse of pink a few feet ahead. As she summons her strength to stand, a sudden shift seizes her muscles. Her body recognizes her mistake.

The wind whips, and the snow dances in front of her. Her breath escapes in desperate puffs as she accepts her fate. The crack and crunch beneath her give way to a dark abyss, a crushing weight so great the air is sucked from her lungs. Marcie kicks and flails.

One last glance towards the white, a spot of pink, one that could never be reached. As Marcie closes her eyes, a feeble voice echoes from the depths.

Let go.

And she is ready. She is ready to give in to the unrelenting wrench of guilt, to free herself from the shackles of grief.

But as Marcie drifts into the undercurrent, an abrupt force draws her upwards. Her skin ignites in the wind, assaulted by the ice. Winnie's yelps encircle her as she is carried toward a faint glowing light. She struggles to keep her eyes open.

"Marcie! Oh God, please...Stay with me, Marcie...please."

Wes's voice is muffled and distant, but his body scorches her through frostbitten clothing. Suddenly, they are inside, the warmth of the living room falling over her like a thick blanket. Her muscles shiver and twitch, her lips tremble, every fiber of her being resonates at an unfathomable frequency.

"Mommy!"

Brayden's frantic cries pierce the haze, but words fail to form in her mouth. Wes lays her onto the tile floor and tears at her sodden shirt. Marcie barely feels the fabric as it's peeled from her numb skin. Panting, he removes the rest of her clothing in a fury, orchestrating her stiff limbs like a puppet master.

When his hands fall on her underwear, Wes stops and turns to Brayden who is standing in the doorway, his eyes swollen with tears.

Wes swallows before addressing his son. "Brayden, buddy, can you...can you go upstairs and grab the heaviest clothes from Mom's closet? A sweatshirt, sweatpants, socks, anything you can find."

Brayden stares at his mother's pale face.

"Okay, buddy?"

He blinks and nods before sprinting down the hallway, a blur of white and brown fur at his heels.

"Marcie? Can you hear me?"

Wes takes her face between his hands, and his palms ignite her cheeks. Marcie's eyelids flutter, and she recognizes panic in his eyes. Her teeth chatter as she mumbles.

"I...I..."

A single tear escapes and falls to the edge of Wes's jaw. "Shh, it's okay. You'll be alright," he reassures her, pushing her cold hair behind her ear. His lips send a ripple of warmth across her forehead.

Wes strips Marcie until only bare skin remains. He pulls a bath towel from the rack on the wall and wraps her in it. Wes holds her tight against his chest, their bodies huddled together on the bathroom floor. Marcie shakes violently as she tries to focus on taking steady breaths.

Brayden stumbles into the bathroom with a pile of clothing. Wes releases Marcie and takes the clothes.

"This is great, bud. Can you get all the blankets together in the living room?"

This time, without hesitation, Brayden runs to the living room. Wes throws the towel aside and dresses Marcie like a doll, her body torpid, her senses muted. He brings her into the living room, placing her on the carpet in front of a crackling fire. In a daze, Marcie watches Wes and Brayden cover her with a mountain of blankets, and she begins to thaw.

Winnie trots over, her snout dusted with fresh snow and a pink prize clutched between her teeth.

Wes reaches out as his eyebrows knit together. "Winnie, what do you have there, girl?"

The dog whines and drops the garment into Marcie's lap.

A child's pink mitten.

Teguin: A Most Unusual Maid

ANN GOETHE

"Stop daydreaming, and do your job."

Teguin dropped the emerald earrings.

Mrs. Allen, the queen's senior housekeeper, stood stiff in her black dress. "What were you planning, to steal those?"

"Of course not."

"Finish your work here in the bed chamber, before moving to the parlor." Mrs. Allen left, shoes clapping against the floor. In her two months since joining the royal household, Teguin had made a fast enemy of Mrs. Allen. "Proud and lazy," the woman often said of her.

Was it possible for a chambermaid to be proud?

Teguin tilted the vanity mirror to clean. She imagined Queen Ardita sitting there, Mrs. Allen brushing her hair. The queen was rumored to be ugly, but Teguin had no proof. A maid could see her sovereign only upon invitation.

"King Regeniere is never at the palace," courtiers whispered. "He finds Ardita's face repulsive."

Teguin knew plenty of village women lacking in beauty but who were nonetheless happily married. Could the king really be so shallow? Or did he keep his distance for another reason, one less suited to gossip?

Her own lips looked colorless, her hair unkempt. Time for some magic. She didn't need to look good for a particular reason. All maids wore the same drab dress and apron. She wanted only an excuse to use her power. To feel the energy surge through her body.

"Flush my lips, and smooth my hair," she whispered to that familiar place in her soul, the place where her magic lived, warm and friendly and waiting. It sprang to life, shooting sparks to her fingers and colors before her eyes. Her reflection changed. Her lips became red, her eyes bright, her hair glossy.

"Saints in heaven."

Mrs. Allen. She had seen the magic, and she looked terrified.

***

Teguin took dinner to her room. Broth, bread, and braised lamb. She could only push wine down her throat. Sip after sip, she waited to feel the drink's effects.

Careless, Teguin thought. Mother's first rule was to practice magic away from prying eyes. Magic was forbidden in the kingdom. If discovered, she'd be executed.

A kitchen maid appeared at Teguin's room. "You're wanted in Mrs. Allen's office." She left without waiting for a response. She set her glass aside and rose. A spell could make Mrs. Allen forget what she had witnessed, but Teguin remembered her mother's second rule: "You must never use your powers to escape life's consequences."

She straightened her dress and walked to the housekeeper's office. "You wanted to see me."

"I've told Queen Ardita we have a witch in our midst." Mrs. Allen sipped from a teacup. "A footman will take you to her rooms."

Mrs. Allen spoke with authority. "I don't expect to see you again."

Teguin followed the footman to the queen's chambers. Without meeting Teguin's eyes, he opened the door and took his post outside the door. She walked inside.

Candle flames danced. Tight curtains enveloped the room in shadows. Her Majesty wore a silk robe trimmed in ermine. The hair on Teguin's neck rose.

"You're a new chambermaid."

Teguin curtsied. "Yes, Your Majesty."

"And you have caught Mrs. Allen's attention. She said that earlier, your appearance changed by...magic."

Teguin kept her eyes down.

"Speak up. I haven't time to dally. Do you have powers, or was Mrs. Allen mistaken?"

"Mrs. Allen was correct. I have powers."

"Where do they come from?"

"Magic might come from an internal or external source, Your Majesty. Mine is internal. It flows in my body like blood."

The queen put a finger under Teguin's chin and forced her gaze up. Teguin saw beady eyes. A long, hooked nose. A mole on the queen's chin, brown and bulbous and sprouting hair. Teguin resisted the urge to turn away.

"You're quite lovely." Queen Ardita released Teguin's chin. "Tell me why you're a lowly servant."

"My mother passed three months ago, Your Majesty. We had no money. The opportunity to work in your household is a blessing."

"In that case, it's only fair that you repay me. I'll not order your death if you give me your beauty."

"I beg your pardon, Your Majesty."

"Your green eyes, black hair, rosy skin." Ardita paused. "You have no need for such traits, but I do. King Regeniere visits tomorrow. We'll begin now."

Teguin's eyes fell on a pitcher and mug. "Your Majesty, please sit at the vanity. I will pour wine for us to share. You must put your lips on the mug where mine were to help the magic flow between us."

"Quickly."

Teguin poured wine and sipped. The queen also sipped, careful where she placed her lips. Teguin bent so the mirror reflected both women. She closed her eyes and spoke to her magic. *I need you.* The familiar tingling took hold, so strong this time it sucked the breath from her lungs. Colors flashed behind her eyes. She murmured an incantation, emphasizing the words *beautiful* and *Her Majesty*.

The rush of magic stopped, retreating to its secret place. The floor dipped. Teguin grabbed a chair for support. When her eyes focused, she saw what the queen saw. Silky red hair spilled over the monarch's shoulders. Her cheeks glowed, her lips looked ripe as peaches. Long lashes framed her eyes. And the mole was gone.

Queen Ardita hadn't changed enough to be unrecognizable, but she certainly looked more pleasing than she had moments earlier.

"My gracious," the queen whispered. Her hand quivered as she touched her face. "The king will be astounded."

The sovereign's eyes narrowed. "I'm beautiful, and you're vile. You fool...you should have chosen death instead."

Teguin knew how she looked to the queen. Double chin, yellow teeth, bald patches on her scalp. And she knew the queen's joy at this turn of events. It vibrated in her voice like a woodwind instrument.

"Leave and tell no one of this."

Teguin curtsied as low as her legs would permit.

***

In her room, Teguin leaned against the door. I've lied to the queen, she thought. She remembered the spell she cast upstairs:

By moonlight's grace,

Give Her Majesty a beautiful face,

But only to her own eye.

And give to me,

An appearance quite ugly,

But change neither in reality.

Teguin couldn't resist a giggle. She'd used her powers to trick the queen. Despite what she thought she saw, her appearance was the same. And so was Teguin's.

But the joy didn't last. Teguin heard her mother's voice. "Never use magic to hoodwink someone in need."

Her mother had hated the idea of Teguin working in the royal household. She pleaded from her sickbed, eager to settle her daughter's future before drawing her final breath. "Follow my footsteps. Use your magic to heal the sick."

Teguin sighed. "Every day, I watch you conjure spells for petty people. Yes, the sick need you, but the others…they use you."

Women came to the cottage, begging for help. "I need to make him love me," one might say. Or "I need to be with child." Selfish, all. But her mother aided anyone who knocked on the door.

"How will you support yourself?" her mother asked.

Teguin could see the hilltop palace from the village. Its ornate towers and stonewalls gleamed in the light. "I'll work in the queen's household."

"You may not get hired. And if you do, you'll never realize your worth under Queen Ardita."

"Oh, Mother…"

She gripped Teguin's hand. "Promise me you'll help others."

Teguin promised. A week later, she wore black to her mother's funeral. She returned to a silent cottage. No fire burned in the grate, no tea brewed in the kettle. When her mother was alive, the cabin had felt warm and cozy. Now it was nothing more than four walls.

Three days later, she ventured to the village square. She wore her mourning dress and slipped two coins into her pocket. It was market day, and Teguin prayed she could afford some food.

"Six eggs for one coin," a farmer cried, his voice rising above the others. The square teemed with people eager to make deals. Teguin pushed through the crowd to reach the farmer. "I'd like six eggs," she said.

The farmer placed the eggs in a basket. "Four coins."

"But you said…"

"You owe me from previous purchases. Wool, oats, cabbage…shall I go on?"

Teguin bit her lip. "Can I pay two coins today and two next week?"

"'Fraid not, Missy." The farmer jerked back the basket, looking for other shoppers.

Teguin turned to leave and bumped a woman. "So sorry," she whispered.

"He's a cold-hearted fool," the woman said with a nod at the farmer. "Anyone can see you're in mourning."

Teguin's eyes filled with tears. "There, now," the woman said. She stroked Teguin's cheek. "I'll bet you need a hot meal and coins for your purse."

Teguin nodded. "Come to my place this evening," the woman continued. "I run a home for young women on Lace Street. I have something you can wear and, if tonight goes well, we'll negotiate a contract."

Lace Street. Teguin looked more closely at the woman's rouge and low-cut dress. Of course, Teguin thought. "Women entertain men in terrible ways on Lace Street," Teguin's mother had said. "You stay away from there."

"No, thank you," Teguin said, jostled by another villager. She wanted nothing to do with a stranger's hands on her body.

The woman grinned. "You'll change your mind."

That night, Teguin sat in bed with her knees up to her chest. A shawl draped her shoulders, two quilts covered her legs and feet. Still, she shivered with cold. In the morning, desperation proved greater than the promise made to her mother. She left the cottage and walked to the palace, fearful that if she didn't, she would end up on Lace Street. And, saints above, Mrs. Allen hired and trained her on the same day.

Now, Teguin wondered if Lace Street would have been the better option. I deceived the queen, she thought. Surely when she finds out, she'll end my life.

***

Teguin rose before the sun. She washed her face and combed her hair; the magic was gone. That place in her soul where it normally lay waiting felt desolate. Like a sky without sun, she thought.

She called upon her magic as she polished the queen's furniture. Not to cast a spell, but to feel the familiar rush of power. To know it was there. To have that secret part of her restored.

Nothing.

She squeezed her eyes until her head ached. *Where are you?*

Nothing.

Mrs. Allen entered the parlor just as Teguin opened the curtains. "What are you doing here?"

"Queen Ardita allowed me to stay."

"I don't believe you." Mrs. Allen grabbed Teguin's arm and dragged her into the queen's bed chamber. "Your Majesty, I found this witch in your parlor. How shall you punish her?"

The queen sat at her vanity, rubbing glycerin into her face. She wore a red velvet gown and freshwater pearls. "You can let her go, Mrs. Allen."

"Are you certain, Your Majesty?"

"We struck a deal last night. As you might have noticed by my appearance, I'm quite pleased with the results."

"As you wish, Your Majesty." Mrs. Allen released Teguin's arm, but not before digging her nails into the flesh. Teguin curtsied and left the room with Mrs. Allen on her heels.

"What is the queen talking about?"

"I wouldn't dare interpret a sovereign's words."

"Answer me."

Teguin thought. "The queen looked happy and well rested, perhaps because the king is coming."

"I am watching you," Mrs. Allen said. "At your very first mistake, I will hand you to the queen for penance. Nod that you understand."

Teguin nodded.

"Finishyour work, and stay out of sight. I don't want you under foot when the king arrives."

"I don't want to be under foot when the king arrives," Teguin murmured.

Mrs. Allen gripped Teguin's shoulders. "Stop being hardheaded. If you do the work required, you can carve a place for yourself here. It's much safer in the palace than out there. What would a girl like you do in the village?"

Teguin saw pity in Mrs. Allen's eyes. "Is that why you're here?" she asked. "Safety from the outside world?"

Mrs. Allen turned away. "Of course not. I'm here because I love the queen."

Teguin heard doubt in Mrs. Allen's voice but held her tongue.

***

After the midday meal, Teguin fled the palace. Some fresh air will clear my head, she thought. She lifted her hem and ran into the forest. She'd been there before, when she needed to escape royal gossip and Mrs. Allen's watchful eye. The towering pines restored her energy.

Now, she removed her servant's cap and let her hair hang down her back. She leaned against a tree, the bark digging into her back. It felt solid and reassuring, like a friend.

How did I weave such a tangled web, she wondered. She tilted her head toward a sunbeam.

"You'll find more sun outside the forest."

Teguin jumped. A man in tall boots stood nearby. He had hair the color of honey and a full beard. His face was tanned, probably from working outside, Teguin thought.

"You seem deep in thought," he said. "Perhaps I should keep walking."

"I am. I was." Teguin pushed her hair from her forehead. "Deep in thought. But the forest is for everyone. You can stay."

He picked a clover from the ground. "It's easy for your mind to wander in a place like this. What's your name?"

"Teguin. I'm a maid in the queen's palace."

"I'm Redge. How do you like the queen?"

Teguin hesitated. I don't know where this man is from. He might be the queen's spy or a thief from the village. She chose her words with care. "I think the more important question is how the queen likes me. To which I might answer not very well."

Redge raised his eyebrows. "Have you done something to offend?"

"I'd rather not say."

"You can trust me."

Redge was older and taller than Teguin. He had kind eyes. His clothes, although simple, looked professionally tailored. "Where are you from?" she asked.

"The countryside, where sheep graze and streams gurgle. Life is simple there, just the way I like it."

"And did you ever do something so foolish, you didn't how to make it right?"

"I will give you the advice my father always gave. Tell the truth."

Teguin imagined telling Queen Ardita about the spell. The queen's look of horror, her hand pulled back to smack Teguin. But with that thought came a tingling in her fingertips, a flash of color before her eyes.

That's it, she thought. Telling the truth will restore my magic.

She sighed. *The truth will also bring my death.*

"What if my confession ends my life?" she asked.

Redge spun the clover in his fingers. "I must take your leave, but perhaps our paths will cross again. In any case, I wish you luck." He bowed and walked out of the forest.

Stay, Teguin nearly called. She hadn't had a friend in so long, and Redge was kind. And handsome. She sighed and placed both hands on a tree, hoping for strength. When she could linger no more, she tucked her hair under her cap and left the forest.

***

In the palace, servants buzzed. "King Regeniere is here," one said. Another shoved white gloves at Teguin. "Put these on and wait at the grand staircase. Queen Ardita wants you to escort her into dinner."

"Why?"

"She said walking next to you will make her look even more beautiful." The maid shrugged. "Why she would think that is anyone's guess. You're stunning."

Of course. The queen wanted a foul-faced maid at her side when she met the king. Never mind that such a display might make Teguin uncomfortable. Anger bubbled in her stomach. "Damn her." Teguin knew cursing the monarch was as good as signing her death warrant, but nobody paid her any attention. The entire staff was busy preparing the royal dinner. Footmen carried meat pies and sugared fruits. Maids wiped glasses until they gleamed.

Teguin slid her hands into the gloves and climbed to the second floor. After a few minutes, Ardita appeared in a champagne-colored gown. Diamonds circled her throat, rubies dangled from her ears.

"Walk by my side to the great hall," she said. "Do not leave until I dismiss you."

Teguin curtsied, eyes on the floor. She walked in step with the queen, her dress occasionally brushing Ardita's gown. At the great hall, two sentries opened the doors. The queen strode the center aisle with confidence. Teguin saw only silk dresses and jewels glinting in candlelight.

They approached the king, seated behind a white clothed table and dressed in a gold overcoat. Teguin glanced his way. Honey-colored hair and beard. She glanced again. Could it be?

King Regeniere was Redge.

Heat flooded her cheeks. What if he acknowledged Teguin? Worse, what if he told the queen of their conversation?

She wanted to flee but watched Ardita take her seat, select her food, sip wine. All that time, she stood behind the queen with her face down. Only after the palate cleanser of sorbet, when the queen finally spoke to her king, did Teguin look up.

"You've said nothing about my appearance. Are you not impressed?"

The king took time with his answer. "I care about your mind, not your appearance. It seems you've not changed since my last visit."

"We haven't spoken since you arrived."

"Did you ask about my mother, who asks after you every day? And where is the hunting dog I gifted you?"

"The dog never stopped barking. I turned it loose."

King Regeniere summoned his assistant. He whispered in the man's ear before answering the queen. "I will leave the palace tomorrow."

"You're supposed to stay a week."

"I cannot be in the same space as you, Ardita. You're selfish to your core."

Ardita sucked in her breath. "All this is for you. This feast, these people, my love. Do you not care?"

King Regeniere sipped from a jeweled goblet. "This is no place for an argument." He nodded at the courtiers, who were pretending to eat but kept glancing at the king and queen. "They'll hear you."

"You," the queen said to Teguin. "More wine."

Teguin reached for the pitcher and leaned over Ardita's shoulder. A ripple of laughter grabbed her attention. Wine poured onto the table, staining the white cloth.

"Fool," Queen Ardita hissed. "What were you thinking?"

Regeniere blotted the mess with a napkin. "It was an accident, I'm sure."

Teguin saw the king's pity, the queen's disdain. Something deep in her belly roared to life. "Your Majesty, I tricked you last night."

Ardita lifted her chin. "How dare you speak to your sovereign."

"The spell I cast did not change your appearance, only your reflection. You're no more beautiful today than yesterday."

"You're lying. I know what I saw."

"When you return to your rooms, the mirror will show your true reflection."

The queen snapped her fingers. "Lock this witch in a cell. At dawn, she hangs from the gallows."

***

Three sentries led Teguin underground, to a cell of stone and dirt. A torch outside the gated door provided the only light. I can get out of here, Teguin thought. Her powers roared to life, casting the cell in a rainbow of color.

Every inch of her body tingled, from toenails to ears. Her confession to the queen had brought back her magic.

But Teguin had learned her lesson. She would follow her mother's rules and cast spells with greater care.

Footsteps. Teguin imagined Mrs. Allen appearing. "The queen doesn't want to wait," she would say. "You're to hang now."

Instead, she saw King Regeniere. He dismissed the sentries and eyed Teguin. "What you did tonight was brave. Foolish, but brave."

"I had to confess."

"The queen says you're a witch."

"I am a witch," Teguin said. "Just as you were born to kingship, I was born with magic in my veins."

"And Ardita asked you to make her beautiful?"

"It's not an extraordinary request, but she's cruel. I'll not help her."

"She's always been selfish. Our parents arranged the marriage hoping queenship would improve her bearing. So far, it's not worked."

"Do you agree I should die?"

The king met Teguin's gaze. He seemed a friendly man, much more so than the queen. Yet he guarded his thoughts. Even with Ardita, he spoke only when necessary. What kind of woman could draw him out, learn his moods and share his ideas? Teguin longed to ask but refrained.

At last, he opened the cell door. "You're a most unusual maid. Leave tonight and don't come back." He pressed coins into Teguin's palm. "Tell nobody you worked here. And saints preserve us, cast no more spells."

Teguin started down the hall but thought of something. "You did a good job concealing your true self in the forest. I could almost think you have sorcery in your blood."

Regeniere grinned. "The queen met her match in you."

***

Teguin held her mother's tarnished mirror. The reflection looked nothing like her but filled her with pleasure. Short blonde hair, blue eyes, freckles. Her high-buttoned dress and matching hat were clean and respectable. Vastly different from when she had worked for the queen.

It felt good to have her magic back. She'd changed her appearance not for vanity but for purpose.

She grabbed her suitcase and left the cottage. No doubt her mother would disapprove, but Teguin couldn't live for her mother. Nor could she abide the king's orders to never again cast a spell. *That's like asking him to stop ruling his kingdom,* Teguin thought.

And yet... she remembered the way he looked at her in the cell. Something had passed between them. Compassion? Understanding? She felt giddy as she walked to the countryside. He said he lived among sheep and streams. She knew the land, had dreamed of it after she left the palace. Her idea was simple: ask for a maid's position with King Regeniere and, after she gained his trust, reveal her true identity. Only to him, of course, and only in want of his friendship.

What harm could come of it?

Teguin saw the king's estate before she reached it. She crossed a wooden bridge and crunched across stone. Met stocky sheep in the meadow and heard a stream splashing against rock. Finally, she reached the estate's front door.

Crows circled overhead. The sun dipped behind a cloud. Perhaps this *was* a mistake. Teguin had no back-up plan if the king's staff was full. What if she had to go to Lace Road and endure men?

The door opened. "How can I help?" a woman in black asked.

Teguin peered. Same voice. Same height. Same dress.

Mrs. Allen.

"Saints in heaven," Teguin breathed. She nearly fled, but her steely core wouldn't allow defeat. Not at this point. Besides, Mrs. Allen couldn't possibly recognize her. She raised her chin. "I'm here to apply for a job." And she waited for the next turn of events.

What She Was

BARB SUMMERS

"Stand still," the mother said, smoothing the girl's savage hair that was as dark as the earth after a storm.

The girl did not like to stand still. The girl liked to run. The girl liked to imagine herself as a wave on the ocean, racing, then crashing and exploding in a glorious spray. The girl would leap into her mother's arms, and the mother would *Oof!* and fall back on her heels and say that it's not lady-like to run in such a manner.

The mother liked the girl to have neat ponytails and clean, shiny shoes. The mother liked for the girl to sit with ankles crossed and hands folded on her lap while politely listening to the teacher and following the rules. The mother knew that a good girl grows into a woman who finds a good man to marry and has her own good children.

The father liked the girl to hold his hand and sit quietly beside him at church on Sunday. It made him feel like a good father. No one saw the empties in the recycling bin or his computer browser's viewing history. Being seen as a good father got him recognized by his boss and promoted, making him a powerful, respected man.

The girl knew nothing of being good; she only knew what she was: the fastest girl in her class and the best tree climber, going higher than the other kids who were afraid. She was smart, she knew where to look when the class's aquatic turtle escaped. She carried him back from the cafeteria, even though he bit her twice. The teacher called the girl audacious and told her parents she had a strong character. So her parents were worried.

The mother and father asked the girl to sit and listen. They tried to explain the parts and pieces of a girl and how, when assembled correctly, a good girl was made. They explained how good girls have good lives with happy parents. It was what they called a *win-win* situation.

"The world is changing," they said, with somber voices. "Life is confusing. But it doesn't have to be, not for us."

The girl saw the earnestness on her parents' faces, saw their clutched hands and pleading eyes. And she heard the whispers from the wind, telling her to run, run, *run*.

The girl wanted her parents to be happy, so she said she would try, while her thoughts were of seagulls and high tides and snaps of lightning across a purply-pink morning sky.

She needed help with goodness, so the mother and father patiently reminded her of all the things she ought to do or, more frequently, the things she ought *not* to do. Day after day their words were a scrubbing brush, sloughing off the bits of her that struggled to behave.

It wasn't long until the girl noticed changes to her legs. They had become hard and heavy, but she wasn't running as much as she used to so she wasn't alarmed. *This must be the type of thing that happens*, she thought.

The mother noticed changes to the girl's hair. Large clumps clogged the bathroom drain and collected like tumbleweed under the girl's bed. The mother assumed it was the extra brushing she encouraged her to do. *She's becoming disciplined*, the mother thought, and she was relieved.

The father noticed changes to the girl's posture. The girl had become straighter and taller. She was almost rigid, and the father told people he encouraged her to walk with schoolbooks on her head. *She's becoming such a prize*, the father thought, and he was proud.

Only the girl saw the thin threads streaming from her toes, a silky gossamer she carefully folded into her shoes every morning, tucking them away along with many cramped feelings that she'd learned to repress.

When the girl stood for long periods on the hill by their house, the mother called her pensive, the father called her demure, and they were assured.

But when the girl took off her socks and dug her feet into the earth and refused to come home for dinner, the mother and father were concerned. Good girls eat dinner at six o'clock. The girl said she wasn't hungry and the mother and father approved of her watching her weight, so they let her be.

When the girl wouldn't come in for bedtime, the mother believed it was because she was praying, and the father believed it was because she was unafraid, so they left the outside light on and went to bed, content in the idea that they were good parents with a good girl.

In the morning, the girl was gone. Instead, there stood a tree at the top of the hill where the girl had been, stretching upward with a hardened spine. The branches drooped, full with blue-green foliage, expanding outward.

The mother asked if, perhaps, they should cry, for it seemed their daughter had turned into a tree. What should good parents do in a situation like this? The father said that he quite liked trees, that they were loyal and picturesque. The mother agreed that yes, trees have a certain something about them. They wondered if their tree would bear fruit.

The tree knew nothing of being good; it only knew what it was: a Weeping Juniper. Tall enough to see the ocean with its cresting waves and screaming gulls.

Make a Wish

MEGGIE ORGAIN

"There's something I want to tell you," I say, fiddling with my ring under the table.

My mother's fork pauses mid-air, carbonara sliding off. "Are you pregnant?"

"No." I slip the ring back into my pocket and incontestably sip my Barolo.

"That's a relief." She chews her pasta.

"Actually, I'm really excited..." I begin my rehearsed speech about the man I love—the one who sends me flowers, changes lightbulbs, and goes to the corner shop for my Snickers.

"I can't imagine what my friends would say," she interrupts, "if they knew you were sleeping around. I raised you better than that." She sips her oaky Chardonnay while I recalibrate.

I give her one last chance. "Remember how I said I'd tell you if I was in a serious relationship?"

"You mean when you forbade me from asking about your love life?"

I look down at my spaghetti. My stomach churns. *More like when you told me it was my fault my ex-boyfriend cheated on me because I gained weight.*

"You can be so spiteful," she continues, "when all I've ever done is love you."

The waiter collects our plates.

She crosses her arms and looks away from me. Several silent moments later, the waiter sets down a slice of cake with a lit candle. She's still looking away; there's no singing. I close my eyes and blow while I wish for my mom to die. So there won't be any questions when I don't invite her to my wedding.

Swimming with the Tide

ANITA JOHN

Will dived in from the rocks and began to swim, his whole body immersed in a fluid silence. When he came up, he felt alive. He started to crawl, breathing out underwater hard and fast so the air from his lungs escaped in a thousand silver bubbles. He lifted his head, first to the right, then to the left on each third stroke, breathed in the sea air, sharp, invigorating, momentary. Then again, three hard strokes. One, two, three, *breath*, four, five, six, *breath*, seven, eight, nine, *breath*. The counting became a mantra, the breathing a meditation which carried his thoughts to another place. An outdoor pool, abroad.

They'd commandeered a derelict house, were waiting for new orders on that heavy summer afternoon. The pool in the grounds looked more inviting than home so when the sergeant gave the go-ahead they all dived in, he and his eleven squaddies. The water was cold. It shocked them into a bout of shouting and splashing, throwing water over each other in great armfuls, diving into the pool like kids. Then the skies opened, and the rain swept over them. They quietened down after that and started to swim, all twelve of them, up and down the pool in unison, side by side as if all their training had brought them to this, as if this was a way of forgetting. Smooth, rhythmical strokes into a liquid which absorbed all deeds, good and bad, valiant and cowardly; into a compound which bound them together, hydrogen and oxygen, in all that they did.

"When your number's up, your number's up," the sergeant had said but what Will *hadn't* done left a niggle, right at the back of his head, which he couldn't scratch away. As he swam now, he counted back the days and knew he should pick up the phone and make *that* call. He'd put it off for days, weeks, months. He swam harder and faster until he felt his lungs burning, then he came up into the sweet, blessed air. Sometimes, you had to face the things that frightened you most. Not guns, not war, not death but people, real, living people. As he turned back for the shoreline, Will heard the voice carry to him in a bluster of wind. "You promised," it said. Overhead, gannets cried and swooped, plunged from on high into the sea.

Commended in the 2014 Words for the Wounded Short Story Competition; published in "The Journey," (White Craw Publishing, 2014) and "Iced Gems" (Self-publishing, 2022). Hardcopies only. Reprinted here with permission from the author.

Unlocked Secrets

CAROL ROEHRIG

Marianne idled her dented Chevrolet in front of a Victorian house set in the middle of an expansive lawn and hovering oak trees. She verified the address on the deed in her hand. The estate attorney had known nothing about this document found in her mother's safe deposit box. She drove around the mailbox and followed the gravel driveway to a parking area.

Why did her mother have the deed for this place? Five white rocking chairs lined the porch below flowering baskets of geraniums and petunias. Marianne clapped the brass knocker against the front door. Hearing nothing, she waited a moment, then banged harder. The sheer curtain was pulled aside in the adjacent window then, with a clatter of keys and locks turning, the door opened.

"May I help you?" A stocky woman dressed in black and white greeted her.

"I'm Marianne Holman. My mother Ruth Holman had the deed for this property in her safe deposit box."

"I'm so sorry for the loss of your mother," the woman replied. "Father Richard from St. Ignatius notified me of her passing. Please come in. I'm Sister Anna. Can I get you coffee or tea?"

"Thank you, a glass of water would be nice."

"Have a seat." Sister Anna motioned to a dark green velvet settee, outlined in carved mahogany.

Marianne surveyed the room: framed oil landscapes on the wall, a dining table surrounded by high back chairs, a crystal vase with freshly cut daisies on the coffee table.

Sister Anna walked with a hobble on her right side. She set a mason jar filled with ice water in front of Marianne and sat across from her.

"How did you know my mother?"

"I met her fifty years ago at St. Ignatius," the nun said. "I taught school there before moving here."

Marianne leaned in. "Why did my mother have this deed?"

"Well, that's a long story. We ran into some financial difficulty, and your mom came to our rescue."

"Who's we?"

"My order, the Sisters of the Holy Trinity. We started this home for unwed mothers seventy years ago."

There was a silence before Marianne spoke again.

"But how did my mother know about this place?"

Sister Anna smiled softly. "Your mother found us not because she wanted to, but she needed to. In her day, women who became pregnant outside of marriage were scorned. Many blamed the young women for being irresponsible. Ruth came here to give birth to you."

Marianne sat back as she remembered her birth certificate from St. Francis Hospital. She brushed hair off her face. "There must be some mistake," she said. "My mother was married to my father when I was born."

Sister Anna unfolded her hands and held her rope belt rosary, searching for a gentle way to share the information that Marianne had been denied.

"Your mother debated telling you." Sister Anna took a long pause, then looked Marianne in the eye. "She was raped after a concert. She came here with the intention of giving up the baby for adoption. Most girls did then. The privacy of unwed mothers was protected by naming St. Francis Hospital as the birthplace on a baby's birth certificate. When your mother decided to keep you, she left us and eloped with Ed. He adopted you."

Marianne sipped from her glass, then circled her index finger around the rim. She crossed her ankles, then uncrossed them. Tears welled in her eyes. Then she got up and paced around the room. Thoughts of betrayal churned in her head. *Is this why I never fit in with my parents? Was my biological father a violent criminal?*

"How could she keep this from me?" Marianne lamented.

"Ruth felt you'd reject her and runaway. She wanted to leave the past in the past."

Sister Anna walked over to Marianne with her arms open. Marianne turned away, so Sister Anna pulled her hands together as if to pray. They shared a gaze.

"I'm so sorry Marianne. Ruth chose to keep you and give you a home that she feared you wouldn't have otherwise. She did what her heart called her to do. I'll pray for your peace and healing." She pulled Marianne in for an embrace; this time, Marianne let her body sink into the caress.

***

Marianne had always known she was different, mainly because she towered above her classmates, topping out at 6'2" in high school. Still, she strode with confidence, oblivious to how she intimidated others. The boys' soccer and track teams accepted her as a teammate for her athletic prowess. Her parents expected her to go to college, find a job, marry a Catholic man, and have children. It's what half the community did.

After high school, Marianne lost interest in sports. She tried community college but grew bored and dropped out. She filled her time with simple hourly jobs. She dreamed of adventure, so one day she walked into a military recruiting office and signed up for the Army, but she grew to loathe the regimented life and left. No matter what she tried, she could not find satisfaction.

Relationships eluded her, too. She dated a tattooed Harley rider, a software programmer, and a business owner fifteen years her senior. Each was more interested in his hobbies or having children than being content with stimulating conversations and companionship. By then, her high school girlfriends were homemakers with children. Marianne babysat a time or two for them, but she could not tolerate all the bickering and neediness. She preferred sitting alone reading or watching classic movies.

***

Sister Anna and Marianne walked through the three-story home, which could house ten clients and two nuns. The home struggled financially. Adoption fees paid most of the costs until those declined because would-be parents went abroad to Chinese and Russian orphanages. When contraceptives and abortions became accessible, fewer young women came to the home. The diocese stopped providing funding.

Marianne turned to the nun and said, "How long ago did my mother help financially, and how much did she give?"

"She has donated to us every year since she stayed here," Sister Anna replied. "Five years ago, I told her we were nearing the end of our financial resources. We had a $300,000 mortgage coming due, and the bank was threatening foreclosure because we had been late with payments."

Marianne frowned. "I didn't know of this, nor did her estate attorney."

"She used proceeds from Ed's life insurance. We had the property assessed, and she paid off the mortgage and gave us $250,000 in cash, which we set up as operating funds."

"Was there a legal document that committed her to keeping the house?"

"We signed an agreement to lease the house for $1 per month for a minimum of ten years. Ruth didn't want a lease, but I needed a document for the diocese and my Order. I'll give you a copy because I doubt she kept one."

"So that means the commitment lasts another five years?"

Sister Anna nodded.

***

Eventually, Marianne found herself back where she had started, at her parents' home. It's possible her mother wanted to escape the small town too, but rape changed everything. Ruth was stuck with a baby and a new husband. She wove herself into a cocoon, rarely hugging or conversing in a deep way. Marianne craved physical touch and meaningful discussions about something other than homework. But now she understood: *How could she hold me close when I reminded her of a violent act?*

One night she looked up in the family den and noticed her mother's journals, bound in floral print. The books filled one shelf and were arranged chronologically. The journals began when Ed died, the writing a way to cope with grief. Most journal entries were prayers asking for God's protection over Marianne and laments about her loneliness. Marianne grew weepy as she studied the beautiful curls, slants, and loops of her mother's expressive pen.

Her parents often sat in lounge chairs separated by a small table with a reading lamp between them. They read in quiet, sipping hot tea, and delighting in each other's presence. At times they would chat about plots or characters, but mostly they turned pages and enjoyed each other. It didn't seem like much fun, yet as she sat in their chairs, she encountered a peace that had eluded her. Words from reading and writing filled the room. Some spoken, most unspoken. There was much about her parents that she had never understood.

***

Marianne walked into Grady Nichols' accounting office; the sweet, earthy aroma of his pipe permeated the space. Wooden floors creaked under her step, while the faint *tat* of computer keys rang in the air. She had not seen him in more than a decade, but his telltale markers remained the same: Navy suspenders stretched over a bunched, white, button-down shirt. The waist band of his khaki trousers rolled over to show the interior white band, his pants at high-water level over black sneakers. It took him a couple of minutes to pull himself up from his chair to greet her. She sat in the guest chair across from him.

"Your father and I were best friends. Not a day goes by that I don't think of him." Grady looked up at the ceiling.

"Dad enjoyed your friendship," Marianne said. "I learned this week that he adopted me. What do you know about that?"

"We had about a year left in our army stint when he came home to visit family and Ruth. They weren't dating, but everyone could see they belonged together. On that visit, Ed learned that Ruth had been raped when leaving a Fair Grounds concert. She only told him. In those days, the shame would have forced her to move away."

"But why couldn't they tell me?" Marianne persisted, expecting to learn more since Grady remained the last connection to her parents.

"As much as Ed wanted to share the story, Ruth didn't want to risk losing you. I can tell you they prayed constantly for you, AND they loved you more than anything."

Marianne looked around, breathing a sigh, and then asked, "Did you know that my mother purchased Bethany Inn?"

"Yes, she consulted with me. I investigated county records and had it appraised. The property was worth more than the money she paid, so whatever happened, it was a sound investment."

Grady told her mother to place the deed in a safe deposit box. Marianne left his office and walked to a park where she sat on a bench and sobbed. *How could they have so much love for me, yet rarely show it? And why didn't we talk about our feelings?*

***

One Saturday afternoon, six weeks later, the doorbell rang. Marianne opened the door to find a tall man dressed in a tapered blue blazer and gray slacks. He had a salt and pepper beard, perfectly trimmed, and square sunglasses propped on his head. It was Ted Krause, her classmate from elementary through high school and favorite soccer friend. He had been the star athlete in their town, a leader in basketball, soccer, and track, and the most sought-after date. Decades had passed since she had seen him, and he was as good-looking as ever.

"Marianne, it's been a long time."

"Of course, Ted. How could I forget soccer and studying together?" She laughed and extended her hand.

"Those were fun times," he said. "I'm wondering if I might talk with you about the Colfax County property." He pulled the sunglasses off his head and folded them into his coat pocket.

"Certainly, come in. Have a seat in the den. May I get you some iced tea?"

"Great, thanks."

He sat on the sofa next to the bay window where the sunlight poured in. Marianne set the tea on the coffee table and turned into the wingback chair across from him. He shared his condolences on the passing of her parents, his kindness showing through as it did when he had helped Marianne with trigonometry.

"I've been in real estate development, and I'm working on retirement housing in Colfax County," he said. "Our firm acquired two farms with contiguous property lines to Bethany Inn. Your land would fill our total acreage needs. I visited with your mother about a sale, but she was not interested."

"I've just become acquainted with the property. I'm not sure what I'll do with it." Marianne got up and filled his glass, noticing his slim build.

"I understand. I'm hoping to put together a county zoning package. It'd be helpful to know if you'd be interested in a sale."

"If I were, when would you take over the house?"

"I'd need to purchase the property and then work on the codes, plans, and approvals. I think it'd take two years before we'd break ground." He leaned forward, watching Marianne's reaction.

"Let me think about it. There are residents in the house that I need to consider."

"Your mother told me about the two nuns. We could set up an apartment for them. I hope you will consider this. I must get going."

He stood to leave, then turned to look around the room.

"It's so warm and comfortable. I bet you enjoy reading here. I remember you loved books."

"I still do and thank you. It's a cozy room." Marianne blushed, flattered by his memory.

***

Sister Anna was cutting roses from the garden when Marianne arrived. After a few days of mulling over her discussion with Ted, she needed to understand how a sale would affect the sisters. It didn't seem sensible for her to hold on to the property.

Marianne picked up the bucket of roses and walked up the back five steps. Sister Anna followed, pulling on the railing as she stepped one foot, then the next, on each stair. Arriving at the landing, she breathed a heavy sigh. Marianne held the door open as they entered the kitchen.

"Would you please put the bucket on the table and pour us some iced tea? I'm very thirsty." Sister moved around a chair, bracing her arms on the table, and sat back. She appeared more fragile than Marianne remembered.

"May I cut those thick stems for you?"

"Wonderful. Here are the clippers and gloves. Watch out for those sharp thorns." Sister Anna handed over the tools as she reached for the sugar.

"Nothing better than some sweet to perk me up."

Marianne chuckled.

"Sister, did you know that a developer is planning a retirement community here?"

"Yes, that's been in the works for years. A couple of farmers sold their property, but they're still working the land. No telling if it'll happen."

"The developer contacted me to see if I'd sell."

Sister Anna sipped tea then set the glass down. She looked up at Marianne. "They contacted Ruth, too. At the time, we had six girls here, and I couldn't imagine what we'd do without this house. Your mother told me not to worry."

She pulled some roses, arranged them in a vase, and continued.

"I never want to leave, but I know that one day I must," the Sister said. "The stairs are difficult with my hip. I'm in my mid-seventies, and I'm not sure where I'd go but I trust the Lord to provide."

"Well, the developer said he'd plan an apartment for you and Sister Bettina."

"See, the Lord is listening. Make sure if this sells, we must find a way to take care of the young women. There aren't many options for them."

After cleaning up the cuttings and placing the vases in the living room, Sister Anna hugged Marianne, a warm and compassionate embrace. Marianne held Sister's hands for a moment, then turned to go to her car. There she found a man in bib overalls trimming the hedges.

"Hello, I'm Marianne. You're always working here."

"Hi, I'm George Nelson. I love gardening and what better way to help Sister Anna? Her kindness and love flow like water down a riverbed."

"So true. Did you know about the retirement project that's planned for here?

"Ah yes. Not sure if it'll happen. It'd be good for more jobs. I'd hate to see these towering trees go. It takes so long to grow these beauties." He drew his arm in an arc and stared at the branches.

"What if they incorporated this house?"

"I care about Sister Anna and that she be taken care of. She's worked too long not to keep her here. She's been good to all of us."

"George, thanks for caring for her. I must get going. Here's my card if I can ever be of help. I'll see you next time."

"God be with you," he said as he took off his glove, received the card, and shook her hand.

***

Sirens blared from every direction, red and blue lights flashing down country roads. A stream of fire engines and ambulances convened in Colfax County. Marianne's heart raced as she shook and prayed that Sister Anna would be safe. George Nelson's phone call had awakened her at midnight with news of a fire at Bethany Inn. Gray smoke billowed above the trees. Marianne screamed in panic.

She parked half a mile away and ran toward the house. Flames were visible near the chimney; part of the roof had fallen in. Sister Bettina was away visiting family, and no guests were in the residence, which meant Sister Anna was alone. Firemen were shouting to one another. Local volunteers held ropes to keep people from danger.

A ladder angled up to a second-story window on the east side near Sister Anna's room. A fireman entered through the window. After five minutes, he shouted for aid in victim removal. Two firemen placed a ladder next to the original one, launched up the steps and quickly moved Sister Anna through the window and down the stairs. The first fireman followed them out. They carried Sister Anna to the waiting ambulance, and it left for St. Francis Hospital. George ran up to Marianne.

"Is Sister Anna okay?"

"I'm not sure, but let's head to the hospital."

Marianne put her head into her palms.

At theEmergency Room, five people were standing around. George Nelson went to the attending nurse to get information.

"She's in the operating room, but her smoke inhalation is severe. The doctors are doing what they can." George took off his hat and rubbed his brow.

"Is there anything we can do?" Marianne asked.

"Sister Anna would want us to pray. There's a group in the chapel if you want to join them. I'll stay here to wait for news."

In the chapel, Marianne knelt while a volunteer led the rosary. It'd been years since she had entered a church, but the words came back to her. Her shoulders shook as she sobbed. *How could such a loving and giving woman face such a tragedy?*

"Please save her, God," Marianne whispered.

After about an hour, George entered the chapel and walked to the front of the room.

"Folks, they tried everything they could, but Sister Anna...." He turned his head up to the cross. "Sister Anna went to the Lord just a few minutes ago. Father Richards arrived in time to give her last rites." He crumbled into a pew and fell to his knees.

A deep hush filled the room. Everyone was stunned. Then a lone voice in the back row began to sing, "Amazing Grace." Slowly voices joined in, followed by another hymn, "Be Not Afraid." Father Richards appeared and walked up the aisle.

"Today we lost our sister, a beloved child of God. She meant a lot to all of us. She'd be delighted to hear you singing. I've been in touch with her order and Sister Bettina. I'll work on funeral plans. We can be ever grateful for her goodness."

He raised his arm and extended his hand in the form of a cross and said, "May the Lord bless and keep you. Amen."

Marianne followed the group out of the chapel, all heads bowed low, no words uttered. George drove her to Bethany Inn, and they stood on the street. The oaks hovered over a charred and smoky structure, a few bits of gingerbread trim still visible, much of the house gray instead of its beautiful lilac. Windows busted out, doors wide open, with pools of water all around the perimeter. Yellow hazard tape encircled the property.

***

One week after the fire, Marianne watched the procession of Sister Anna's casket to the altar of St. Ignatius Church. A soprano sang "It Is Well With My Soul," stirring Marianne to tears with the lyrics. She knelt in the pew and stared up at the red, blue, and yellow prism of color from the stained glass as it danced on the altar. The words evoked images of her mother writing prayers, and George's description of Sister Anna's kindness. The sweet cedar scent of incense invited her back to a place that felt like home.

***

A couple of weeks after the funeral, Marianne contacted the insurance company to review the claim process. The adjustor worked with the fire chief and determined the cause was lit candles that had fallen from a table and burned draperies. The structure could not be restored, and they recommended bulldozing the building and laying a new foundation. The adjustor said the claim would be processed in a month with a payout adequate to rebuild Bethany Inn.

***

Marianne contacted Ted Krause and met him at his office to discuss the sale of the Bethany Inn property.

"Ted, I'm ready to sell the Colfax County acreage, so I need a formal offer. Before you do so, however, I have a contingency that I want as part of the sale."

She sat upright and leaned in toward his desk.

"I want to continue the mission of Bethany Inn. I envision a separate adjacent building called Anna's Family Center. This facility would help young people by providing sex education, rape and trauma care, along with prenatal and post-birth housing for unwed mothers. Professionals from St. Francis would manage the facility, with an invitation for elderly residents to help young mothers and guide them in the proper feeding and nurturing of infants."

"I'll consult with my partners and see what we can do," he said.

***

Holding the deed, Marianne settled into the reading chair. She thought of her mother's courage to keep a child she could have left behind. The trauma impeded her openness with fear that the truth could upend what she loved, a daughter and a husband in a quiet home life. Violence took away her ability to let go and release the love she held so carefully. *She loved me with quiet, deep, abiding compassion. I wanted more, yet she gave me everything she had.*

The building of Anna's Family Center would become her way to honor the legacy of her mother and Sister Anna. Finally, Marianne discovered her destiny to give to others what her life represented, redemption from violence to love. *Mother would love to see me carrying on her legacy.*

Marianne brushed her hand across the spines of the journals that honored the years of Ruth's grief. She pulled down a blank book and sat in the comfortable chair. There, she began to move her pen across the page, writing of gratitude for her mother's love and grief in losing her. She then composed a prayer of thanksgiving for the gift of unlocked secrets.

The Project

MEGGIE ORGAIN

5:42 am

Katie cradled a warm mug of coffee in her hands and blinked at the sudden brightness of her computer. Screw whoever said the best time to work was before everyone else was awake. But they weren't wrong, were they? When else would she have time to focus on this project?

She couldn't work on it yesterday because it was Wednesday, and while Wednesdays weren't as crazy as they used to be (ever since she'd pulled her middle child, Gracie, out of gymnastics), there was still soccer for her oldest, Sammy, manhandling the other two kids on the sidelines, and the mad dash home afterwards for dinner and bath time. So it must've been Tuesday that she'd last looked at it.

But that can't be right because Tuesday Tyler, her youngest, required extra attention as he was still coughing everywhere except into his elbow (although at only two years old, could she really blame him, when his 35-year-old dad still couldn't remember to wash his hands after he took a shit?).

All that to say, it had been more than two days since she'd worked on it—which might as well be two years with how well her brain retained things these days. Like a colander holding water.

She sipped her coffee. Focus. Open the anonymous browser. What was next on the checklist?

Reviews, she needed to read reviews. It wasn't enough anymore to go in blind on a purchase, especially one this important. No, she had to look at the reviews, so she knew what she was getting. Unlike marriage. There were no reviews she could've read before her wedding. At least not for the groom.

Should she start a load of laundry? If she started now, she could switch it over when the kids were getting ready for school and then start the next load. And the next and the next and the next. Until all the clothes were clean and all she had to do was fold and put everything away.

But all of the kids' hampers were in their rooms. Wouldn't waking them up to get their laundry sort of defeat the purpose of this early morning work session? Should she risk trying to get her and Mike's hamper from their room? Sure, if it was their toddler screaming bloody murder in the middle of the night, he couldn't be bothered, but he'd wake up as soon as she opened their door.

No, the laundry could wait.

The letters on the computer screen blurred together. What had she been reading? She rubbed her eyes and read again. Better, sort of. It was hard to see because she was sitting in a dark room looking at a dark screen with blinding white letters on it. That couldn't be good for her eyes. Or anyone's. Didn't doctors say looking at screens all the time was scrambling their brains? They're probably right. They were doctors after all.

She should limit Tyler's screen time more. He's watched at least one movie every day since the start of the school year when the two older kids stopped providing entertainment—or at least a distraction—during the day. Summers with three kids at home all day (with the cost of summer camp, who could afford to send them anywhere?) were hard but being home alone with a toddler during the school year was harder. No matter how each day started (trip to the park, library story time, arts and crafts project), she would eventually give in (let him watch a video on her phone, play a game on the iPad, park him in front of a TV movie). Screens were easier than starring in a one-woman show, *Staying Home with Your Kid.*

And why should she be the only one who took her job seriously, anyway? But sure, she should probably work on limiting screen time.

Scratch, scratch, scratch.

Was that Murphy pawing at the bedroom door? That damn dog better not wake up Mike. Or else she really would leave him by the side of the road this time. Sure, it had been her idea to rescue him in the first place (*It's good for kids to have a pet—they can learn about responsibility and the cycle of life!*), but now he was just one more creature she had to pick up after. That was probably too harsh. She loved Murphy and his crooked little ears. But really, she should let him out of the room before he woke Mike. She couldn't deal with her husband yet.

Even if this project was all about him.

6:23 am

Murphy was curled in a black and white ball at Katie's feet, released from his prison of the bedroom. She sipped her second cup of coffee (and she wondered why she felt anxious in the morning—couldn't be the acidic, caffeinated beverage she drank on an empty stomach, could it?) and pulled up the forum she'd been perusing before the damn dog distracted her.

Ahh yes, there was the thread she'd found last week. Honest reviews. But how honest were they, really?

Take Katie. If you asked her to review her life, she'd say, *Great! 10/10 would recommend!* She wouldn't say, for example, that most days, she couldn't keep a single thought inside her head for more than a fleeting instant before the next one came crashing in like a train rolling down the tracks, unstoppable and impossible to ignore.

She also wouldn't admit that she was tired, so very tired. Not the normal I-have-three-kids-and-haven't-slept-enough-in-years tired. No. A level of exhaustion had seeped into her very soul that made her question if this was real life or some crazy simulation run by an evil billionaire that everyone around her was unwittingly participating in. And she certainly wouldn't say that she couldn't remember the last time she had done something she wanted to do. She couldn't even say what that was anymore. Just that she hadn't been able to do it in a very, very long time.

Not since before Sammy was born seven years ago, and she and Mike had decided she would stay home because her salary was smaller than his and she was the one feeding the baby from her body, so it just made sense, right? Because childcare was too expensive and moms were hardwired to be better caretakers than dads, and if her body was the one that needed time to heal, then she should stay home and not worry about pumping in a bathroom or using up her PTO on sick kid days, and did they really want strangers raising their baby anyway?

So they struck a deal. Mike would work and take care of their family. He was a successful software salesman and would earn the money, do what he needed to do to provide for his family, and Katie would stay home with Sammy (and then Gracie, and then Tyler). Eventually they would be able to afford childcare, if Katie ever wanted to return to work. It was her choice—totally her choice!

Yes, reviews were important, but you had to remember they never told the whole story. She focused on her computer screen. Had she been reading the review by Maverick6219 or darkvaness2? Maverick was complaining that his refund request had been ignored for days. That was a red flag and, wait, the next review said the same thing! Well, that site must be a scam. Glad she hadn't fallen for it. Surely there were better options. Just keep scrolling.

Cough, cough.

Katie looked at the two baby monitors next to her laptop to see which one lit up. Please don't let it be Tyler, he was just starting to get better and if this cough plus post-nasal drip turned into a full-blown ear infection, that would be his fifth this year and the pediatrician said they would need to see an ENT because he might need to get tubes put in.

Please not Tyler, please not Tyler.

On the other hand, it wouldn't be the worst thing if it were Tyler since he wasn't in school anyway. It's not like another kid would be at home with her; just business as usual. Plus, if he did need tubes, they'd already met their insurance deductible for the year (although there would still be co-pays and how many more appointments?), so it might not be so bad to go ahead with the surgery. Assuming they could get it scheduled fast enough (and assuming she could figure out how to pay for the portion insurance wouldn't cover).

She'd heard horror stories of long waiting lists and calling in favors from friends of friends. She didn't have friends of friends.

She clicked on the video monitor. There was her baby boy, spread eagle in his crib, sound asleep. Maybe it was a one-off cough. She set the monitor down and turned back to her laptop.

Cough, cough, cough. Mommyyy. Mooommmyyy.

The lights on the sound-only monitor lit up as Katie's four-year-old daughter called to her. Gracie. Why couldn't she wait just a little longer for the time-to-wake clock in her room to go from red to green? Well, there was no point trying to work on the project now. It would be impossible to get Gracie to stay quiet in her bed for the next fifteen minutes and not wake her brothers. May as well start the morning routine.

Maybe she could work on the project during Tyler's afternoon nap. Assuming he took a nap. He'd been refusing it lately and some days just sat in his crib and screamed for an hour. Not that she let him scream for a whole hour. She wasn't a monster or anything. She cared about creating a secure attachment and all those things the toddler books talked about. But she wasn't ready to give up on the nap. It was the only time in the day she could catch her breath. So she'd let Tyler cry and yell for ten minutes and then go into his room, pick him up to calm him, and set him back down in his crib. Over and over and over until "nap time" was over and she was a grumpy, tired mom with a grumpy, tired toddler, so she'd turn on the TV and tell all those doctors to shove it because her brain was already scrambled and who the hell cared anyway?

Cough, cough, MOMMYYY!!!

Mamaaaaaa.

Shit. Now both Tyler and Gracie were awake. She just had to get through the next twenty minutes. And then the next hour. And the four hours after that. And then maybe she could work on this project again.

She closed the browser and shut her laptop.

12:51 pm

Sammy and Gracie were at school (thank goodness Gracie's cough was just a response to the recent cold front and not because she was actually sick). Tyler was asleep. At least Katie believed he was. He'd protested his nap for a solid 20 minutes before he finally laid down in his crib.

Ahh, if only the hardest thing Katie had to do today was fall asleep. Toddlers were such assholes. Too harsh? Maybe. If she focused for half an hour right now, she could probably put a dent into the project and still have time to eat a quick lunch while folding laundry before he was up again. She set a timer to keep her on schedule.

Enough with research and reviews—she needed to commit and get the ball rolling. She'd already established her budget and squirreled away the money bit by bit (mostly by paying less to their joint credit cards each month—at this point, who cared if they incurred a little more debt? It's not like Mike would notice). She needed to decide on a vendor and details.

First there was the question of when. The holidays were right around the corner and she needed the project done before then. From an economic perspective, it would be helpful to have an extravagant expense like this over and done with so that she wasn't tempted to use any of these funds to buy the kids' presents.

And considering the financial predicament they were currently in, things would definitely be tight. At least until the project was finished. Plus, all the lights, Santa visits, and parties could provide a much-needed distraction for the kids.

But when?

Next weekend they had Sammy's soccer tournament, the one after was the school carnival she'd volunteered for, and the one after that was the park birthday party for Gracie's friend.

Why was she only looking at weekends? A weekday could work. Mike had that conference coming up at the end of the month. She should probably wait until he was home from that, right?

Wasn't this what Mike always complained about? Her indecisiveness, being wishy-washy. Well, maybe he'd have trouble deciding stuff too if that's all he had to do all day. Like what's for breakfast, or how much should she sell Gracie's old clothes for on Facebook Marketplace, or when should they leave for soccer practice, or which bill could she put off until the next paycheck, or why is the ice maker still making that weird sound even though they'd called two handymen and a plumber who all said it was working just fine?

She hadn't always been like this—second-guessing every move she made. She'd made choices back when she still believed she had choices to make. Mike had promised that if she stayed home and took care of the kids, he would take care of the finances. And he had, for a few years.

Then the pandemic hit. And honestly their family had it easy, didn't they? No one got really sick, none of their family died, and Mike didn't lose his job. He still brought home a paycheck; it just wasn't as much as it used to be. That wasn't his fault; it turned out that data analysis software wasn't an "essential" expense for most companies. And sure, the timing of Gracie's birth in March 2020 probably couldn't have been worse, but how do you plan for something like a once-in-a-century health crisis?

Times were tough for everyone though, weren't they? So Katie had dug in, doubled down on taking care of the family. She overhauled their household budget, bought store-brand paper products, learned to appreciate the work Mike was doing for their family. And things got better.

For a while. Then Katie had run the numbers and told Mike their family (and therefore, their expenses) had grown, but their bank account had shrunk. She wanted to go back to work. It would be best for all of them.

But he'd disagreed.

Who would hire her? With the gap in her résumé and the flexible schedule she'd need to pick up the kids from daycare, there weren't many options.

Fewer, still, who could pay her enough to actually cover the expense of childcare?

He'd said the job market had shifted to remote work post-pandemic, and he supposed she could look for something part-time to do at home while staying with the kids. If she really wanted to. But he was also working from home a lot and it wasn't like they had two home offices, so for the time being she should focus on her **real** job—their family.

Plus, he had some investments lined up that were going to pay out big in the future. Huge. The money would come soon. She'd see

Beep, beep, beep. Beep, beep, beep. Beep, beep, beep.

Had it already been 30 minutes? And she still hadn't made a damn decision. Okay, fine. The week after Mike's conference; she could offer a few dates. She'd try to squeeze in some more planning during screen time after she got the kids from school. Progress had been made; just a few more details.

3:23 pm

Aladdin was on the TV, Sammy was fighting aliens on his tablet, and popcorn was on the coffee table. Katie only had a few minutes. She opened her laptop at the dining table where she had a clear view of her children. The *when* had been decided; now she needed to choose the *where*.

They could do it at the house, but it was hard to clean up with three kids under foot, and who knew what the place would look like after?

His office? The parking garage? The coffee place just beyond their neighborhood?

She needed to decide. Except maybe she didn't. Isn't that why you hired professionals? So maybe the next step wasn't choosing *where* it would happen, but just the *who*.

Her gut was telling her to go with the one she'd read about last week. The reviews were all positive, if not totally over-the-moon. Maybe she should keep looking. Maybe there was something better out there.

"Decision fatigue" they called it. But it was more than fatigue now, wasn't it? More like decision rage.

Mommy, can I have another snack?

She would go with her gut. It was about time she started listening to that again. Although the last time she did, she'd ended up pregnant with Tyler. It was right after Mike had rejected her desire to go back to work. He was in charge of bringing home the bacon; she was in charge of the little mouths who ate it. And after Mike went back to playing golf at the club with "potential customers" and hiding out in deer blinds with "referral sources."

With all other options off the table, and what looked like more money coming in, soon, what decision was there to make? One more little mouth would mean one more chance to show how good she was at her job. On second thought, maybe that wasn't her gut speaking after all.

Mom, my iPad died, where's the plug?

She would put down a deposit and message the admin, asking for professional input on the details. Everyone was always telling her to delegate more anyway. Wasn't that what this whole project was?

Mama, where Elmo? Elmoooo!

Gracie needed more snacks, Sammy needed a charge, Tyler needed his furry red stuffy. She would have to wrap this up tonight after the bedtime rush. Tell Mike she had to read some gentle parenting blogs. Not like he'd even notice her absence.

Unless he got hungry.

8:49 pm

Kids in bed? check.

Dog fed and let out? check.

Mike mindlessly scrolling Instagram? check.

Katie didn't even need to make an excuse; she got up and walked out of the living room. But what if he walked in and saw what she was working on? Was he suspicious? Of course not. That man wouldn't know a secret was brewing if it tore his pants off and blew him right there on the couch.

She opened her computer. Head down, focus. Open the anonymous browser, find the address, enter it into her wallet. Why did she need to approve the transaction so many times? Yes, this was her money to spend (even if it probably should've been spent on credit card debt). Yes, she wanted to do this (there wasn't another option, was there?). Yes, she was sure (right?).

Then why was her heart racing?

Hey, babe?

It was ironic, wasn't it? That she was paying in the same cryptocurrency that had led her down this path to begin with. It had started (continued? progressed?) when she noticed the biweekly deposits from Mike's paycheck getting smaller. When she asked, he'd explained the company was restructuring their compensation package to include a smaller base salary, but bigger commissions on sales. So it might hurt a bit at first, but the potential upside was way better.

Then she started getting the collections calls.

Katie just needed to type out the admin request, and her work would be finished. *Need this done week of November 4th. Open to ideas on location and exact day. CanNOT be at home.*

Babe! Did you get my dry cleaning?

The investments Mike had lined up that were supposed to pay out were in Bitcoin. Which would have been fine, until he started leveraging for larger positions and all their savings had been liquidated. Gone. He'd thought he could fix it, which is where the new (immediately maxed out) credit cards came in. The first couple under his name, the next four under hers.

She typed: *Target is Mike Milner (35 yo) in Frisco, Texas.*

I have that meeting tomorrow, and I need that shirt! Where are you?

Mike was supposed to supply the money, take care of the finances. That was his end of the deal. While Katie shopped at thrift stores, sold baby gear, and took Gracie out of gymnastics, Mike was buying new golf clubs and gambling away their future.

When she confronted him, he hadn't even apologized. Just said, *Don't worry, I'll take care of it!*

Like he'd taken care of everything else?

Katie's credit score could probably recover if she paid off the cards soon, but with no job and no prospects, where would she get that kind of money?

No sense in divorce; aside from the house (plus the monthly mortgage insurance payments), there was hardly anything to split up. Plus, the idea of letting that selfish asshole share custody of their kids—no. She would hold up her end of the deal. She would take care of her family.

Babe? Why didn't you get my dry cleaning today?

The only thing still worth anything was the life insurance. Because paying bills was her job, and she'd never missed a premium payment.

She finished typing: *It needs to look like an accident.*

I told you I needed that blue striped shirt for my meeting tomorrow.

Sorry, babe. The day got away from me.

Mike stood in the doorway behind Katie. Had he seen what she was working on?

I guess I'll go find a different shirt. He walked away. Down the hall, she heard him muttering, *What do you even do all day?*

Katie clicked submit. The project—the hit she'd just ordered—was out of her hands now. She'd taken care of the problem.

Poetry

Her Sex Life in 5 Sentences

MANDY PRELL

Everything melts together in a pleasant and familiar way, but he is
her family now,
not her lover.
She wants a rising, feral madness palpitating in her chest. She wants to feel the heat of his boiling blood, enraged and unleashed at the sight of her bare inner thighs, as if her legs are a feast for his consumption.
She wants
delicious,
impulsive,
exploratory
ecstasy.

Perhaps, after she puts the kids down for bed,
they can both get high enough to forget
she is Mom.

Tracing

APRIL KRASSNER

Genealogy is complicated
and that beautiful man
with dark hair and blue eyes
could be, but isn't, Dutch.
It is what adoption gives us,
complication and remove.
He told me, that man I know,
the one with the skinny ankles
and white socks, blue eyes,
dark hair, a sleeve tattoo, that
his father is adopted, and I thought
of my daughter, who does not want
to have children, what it means
to have a last name like mine born
from a ninety-eight percent certainty
of who I am, yet she isn't.
What a beautiful man, she whispered.

He stood smiling, tattooed sleeve
showing. My daughter likes tattoos,
carries a spider inked into her arm,
my ancestors had numbers stamped
into theirs. That beautiful man
and my beautiful daughter both carry
sorrow for the unknown
and a determination to be seen.

Sixteen

ANITA JOHN

There was that day in May during study leave
when you asked if we'd like to go for a walk.

We packed cheese and ham sandwiches,
three oranges, some chocolate
and flasks of water and juice.

We'd walked these fields
for more than sixteen years, and yet
you showed us your own path
from Kitleyknowe to Carlops.

We skirted Mill House, climbed
Patie's Hill and watched the view steadily open –
Lammermuirs and Moorfoots to the south-east,
Pentlands firmly under our feet.

You asked why the earth was spherical
and whether there was an easy
explanation for gravity

then turned, like the wheeling gulls,
to trace the line you'd taken winter sledging,
the place you'd baled out – where hill
plunged to burn and fence wire.

You explained the qualities of snow,
how jump skis differ from slalom skis,
how, come winter, you'd travel to France,
train as a ski instructor.

We settled back in the wind-blown grasses,
absorbed the rare and sun-soaked afternoon,

listened to meadow pipits, crows, gulls,
the whisper of water under the bridge.

Your voice danced, light as the orange-tip
butterfly, newly emerged,

making us forget the journey's doubt,
uniting mother and father
with their last-born child,
their late-born boy.

Highly commended in the Gerard Rochford Poetry Prize 2021 and published on September 27th 2021 at: https://www.facebook.com/GerardRochfordPoetry/

Lingering Effects

MANDY PRELL

I almost die choking on a cold French fry from Penn Station—aglow from warm light underneath the microwave, eating *leftover* fast-food above the stove in the dark like a rat. Calm attempts to restore oxygen fail and genuine fear supersedes the humiliation of motioning my husband from the patio. Several full-bodied slaps on the back dislodge a bit of potato from my throat. Tears stream as the coughing fit subsides.

When I realize I'm going to live, I think: *This is punishment for considering divorce.*

I Only Have Memories

DEENA STAPLES

Dad's hair is completely silver. It's no longer the black-brown of my childhood, when looking up at his face took effort because I was small and he was tall. The hair that my dad loved to have my sister and I comb, wind around curlers or put up in butterfly clips. No longer just a sprinkling of gray that he said we gave him, this silver is the color of a life lived, long days of work, watching his own father die and his mother age, walking his daughters down the aisle, becoming a grandfather six times over and now, caring for my bedridden mother.

It's not the color of his hair that knots my throat. He looks sophisticated, his thick hair the color of tinsel and parted to one side. What pulls at my heart is that I am not a child anymore—now I have a sprinkling of gray. Time is running out. As a little girl, I was happy with small snippets of my father's attention, but as an adult, I am hurt that I have only memories. His gray hair tells me we are running out of time, that the one thing that holds us together, my mother, will soon be gone.

It Was Difficult to Reach the Summit; This Is What It Took

April Krassner

                        She tells us

she is confident anyone can do

    what she has done, that it's not

    that hard, if they follow instruction

    on the raising of goats. She says

    she has written six books mostly

    about goats.

                        In my family

    we are afraid, my niece

    crying over goats and the bumps

    on their heads while others

    clamor, *Look at the goats, look*

    at the goats when it is sheep

they are petting.

                                   We just
never learned to know
animals, farms, or how
things grow. We raised
ourselves in the wilds
of suburban space behind homes,
schools, and parks.

                                   For us,
the natural world was built
in rose bushes planted
along fences, flower beds shared
between houses. Weeds sprang up
from the cracks of the sidewalks.

                         Step on a crack,
break your mother's back,
we'd chant knowing nothing
of the wildness of a nature
red in tooth and claw. Our songs
of experience manufactured and tamed.

                      The unleashing
always came from the fathers
just back from war, carrying
their rage home after marching

in formation through field and marsh

seeing atrocities they would never forget.

Three Friends

DEENA STAPLES

Tails wag and thump
  against the door. One
  tan, one chocolate,
  one brindle. It's too early and
  I am slow to react,
  kept up late by the heat
  of my aging body.
  I turn the door knob and they jump,
  sniffing patches of ground,
  excited to greet the day
  and whatever emerged
  overnight. The earth is covered
  in a fine mist that dampens
  my slippers. They are unbothered
  by the cold, but it stays with me
  long after we come inside,
  my body never knowing what

temperature it prefers.

The four of us rest on the loveseat

that's just for them. One on each

side of me, the little one in my

lap. I close my eyes and take a deep,

grateful breath.

Creative Nonfiction

A Solo Traveler

LIWEN

On a crisp fall morning two years ago, I was journaling in the garden of a museum on the Upper East Side of Manhattan. The leaves were falling; the ground was a mosaic of red, orange and yellow and the sky was as clean and blue as a baby blanket. But inside me swirled a torrent of fear and anxiety. In the middle of a divorce, I was afraid of living alone, making decisions on my own, and desperate to feel loved.

Writing became my daily therapy.

Within my sight line, a family of four were looking for a table. I gave mine to them, and took a smaller one. Their sons, a few years older than my teenage boys were at the time, pulled out a deck of cards and started playing with their parents, chatting in a language I couldn't discern. The wind started picking up. They buttoned up their jackets, held tight to the cards, not giving up their game.

My eyes grew misty. A family activity so small, calm, and ordinary was absent from my life.

Curiosity overtook emotion, and I asked, "What language do you speak?"

"It is Danish. We are from Denmark," the younger-looking son, who wore a lavender hoodie and a nose ring, replied with a big smile.

"Oh, the land of happiness," I said.

"Where are you from?" the woman with glasses asked in a gentle voice, her lips curling into a half-moon.

"China, but I live here," I answered.

Four pairs of eyes widened with excitement.

"I love China," the older son jumped in. "I am going to backpack in China."

In 10 minutes, we bonded like old friends. Lone, the mom, worked in a high school in Aarhus, Denmark's second largest city after Copenhagen. One of her favorite projects was to initiate and organize cultural exchanges for her high school students in foreign countries. Jens, the husband, was a science professor. He didn't talk much but had a constant smile, eager to please and connect. Joakim, the younger son, was going to take a gap year before college. On top of free education and healthcare, his government would pay him a few hundred dollars a month for simply being a college student.

"You young Danes are so spoiled," I teased.

"I would love to visit Denmark," I added, sharing that I'd been traveling solo for a year, fascinated to learn what makes people happy. After a few more minutes of chatting about New York City's high rents and skyrocketing college tuition, the family disappeared in the autumn breeze in search of Levain Bakery's cookies, my recommendation.

A week later, Lone texted me: "If you ever come to Denmark, we have an extra room for you."

I stared at the screen, all tears. At the most painful time of my life, my heart longed for generosity, tenderness, and affection. When romantic love ended, another kind of love, love for self and human connection, started taking hold.

For twenty years, I traveled frequently between Asia and America with my ex-husband and my sons. Never did I worry about missing flights, getting sick or having my wallet stolen. Now, that's all I think about before each trip. Mishaps during travels seem four times larger when I am alone. I wonder how my mind can play such tricks on me.

"The only way to conquer fear is through action," I tell myself.

I started by taking baby steps, applying for writing workshops overseas. In March 2024, I was thrilled to be accepted to a program in Iceland. Gazing at Google Maps, I was part excited, part fearful. I wanted to go somewhere else after spending a few days with other writers in the capital city of Reykjavik, but where would I go?

Denmark is basically next-door. And I know people there!

"Hey, I am coming to Copenhagen!" I texted Lone.

"Come to visit us. I can pick you up at the airport," she texted back. As if she could read my mind, another message followed: "It is very safe for women to travel alone in northern Europe. Our neighbors don't even lock their doors at night."

Was I ready to stay with a family I barely knew in a foreign country? I would not do this if I were still married. Now, single, I make my own decisions. I want to feel what I felt 27 years ago when I arrived in the United States not knowing anyone. Back then, there was no fear, only joy, excitement, and hope.

"Yes, I am coming!!!" I ended the message with three exclamation marks.

One and a half years after I met the Danish family in New York, my plane touched down in a small airport I had never heard of.

It was late. After collecting my bags, I stepped outside to the pick-up area, anxiously scanning the unfamiliar faces.

Lone was waiting. Shorter than I remembered, she had the same half-moon smile.

"The teachers in my school think I am crazy picking up a woman from NYC to stay with us," she joked.

"My friends think I am crazy too," I replied. "But I would have never done this if a guy had invited me. No matter how hot he is."

 We burst into laughter.

It was pitch-black outside. For most of the 90-minute drive, we were the only people on the highway. Gone was the trepidation I felt post-divorce about visiting a foreign country. The image of her family playing cards in the wind was forever inked in my mind. I let myself sink deep into the seat, feeling at home.

We arrived in a picturesque eco-village 15 minutes outside Aarhus, a diversified community of about 300 people.

"We choose to live here because we believe in shared resources and helping each other," Jens said. Residents have the option to share cars, bikes, and electric tools; they take turns caring for the disabled and cook for families a few times a month in exchange for dinner prepared by others the rest of the month.

In the village center, there was a convenience store stocked with eggs fresh from chickens raised in the village, home-made ice-cream by a famous chef, and fresh pastries baked by village residents. Pick what you want, pay as labeled. All on the honor system.

I was amazed by how the Danes trusted each other. Full names were carved outside their doors, some even with phone numbers on them. Forget about the things I was told bring happiness: candles, bath salts, fuzzy blankets.

The Danes were happy because they trusted each other. And I was a beneficiary of that trust.

At the north end of Denmark is a beach town called Skagen, known for a powerful image of a stretch of long white foam created by the North Sea clashing and merging with the Baltic Sea. On the same beach, 130 years ago, the Danish painter P.S. Kroyer painted his masterpiece depicting two women engaging in a quiet conversation after sunset. The scene was rendered in soft blue tones, creating a serene and nostalgic atmosphere. The beach stretched far into the background, and the sea appeared calm and peaceful, with the sky and water blending seamlessly.

Lone and I loved this painting. I loved the blue hour when the sea and sky dissolved into a mist of indigo. I wondered what the women were chatting about.

"Lone, let's pretend we are the women in the painting. Let's have our photo taken from behind, just like them," I said.

We circled our arms, sauntering towards the sunset, while Jens studied the painting, adjusted his camera lens, and took a modern-day "Women on the beach in Denmark."

I marveled at the magic of nature, of random encounters, and of the curious ways we bumped into each other's lives. Humans are wired to connect, to love and be loved. On that cool morning in New York City two years ago, I felt fear and longing. Now that fear is washing away. I feel young again, full of joy, love, and adventure.

Glass

JULIE SONG

I dashed off a text to my friend Leona back in California. *We just got home from The Jersey Shore, and now these crazy fools are going swimming. Would it be messed up if I told them I'm going to the library?*

Leona responded with three large crying-with-laughter emojis. A beat passed before her second text came in.

Fake a headache, and lock yourself in the bedroom.

The texts were a soft chisel against a frosted window that chipped away at my icy frustration that had thickened over the past few weeks. Her grace and humor cracked away at it, letting slivers of light spill through, melting away my tension.

We were at the tail end of our annual monthlong visit to my in-laws on the East Coast, a trek we made every summer since our son Benji was born seven years ago. Living on the opposite coast, we rarely got to see Mike's side of the family, and we wanted to make sure Benji had ample time with his paternal grandparents, cousins, aunts, and uncles. So for the past eight summers, we'd packed our laptops to work remotely, along with clothes and books, and flew across the country to stay with Mike's parents.

My in-laws' expansive home in Pennsylvania was worlds apart from our modest house on the edge of Los Angeles. With seven bedrooms, there was ample space for everyone to spread out. My father-in-law, whom we affectionately called "Pop Pop," devoted his summer afternoons to mixing elixirs of chemicals to ensure that the water in the pool, jacuzzi, and hot tub sparkled. In the family room, a half-completed puzzle was always laid out on a fold-out gaming table, where people would stop to lock a piece into place. Books read over decades filled the oak shelves, and a lifetime of photographs lined the walls. It wasn't the home I grew up in, but it was cozy as a soft sweater on a brisk autumn morning.

After a few days, we piled into our rented minivan and made our way through five states, from Pennsylvania to Massachusetts, where we spent every Fourth of July with my mother-in-law, Nancy, and her family. Ellen and Bill, her sister and brother-in-law, hosted 30 to 40 family members at their house on the water, filling our days with fresh lobster dinners, flowing cocktails, kayaking, and paddleboarding in the calm, cerulean bay. We played corn hole and bocce ball on the sprawling lawn. A steady rhythm of small talk, game-playing, snacking, and drinking filled our days. On our final night, fireworks shattered the inky sky, reflecting glitter in the water below. Adults and kids alike danced with sparklers, lit fireworks, and swatted away "no-see-ums," invisible bugs who pierced our skin with sharp stingers.

A blanket of melancholy weighed heavily over our drive back to Pennsylvania. Pop Pop was the one brave enough to vocalize our thoughts.

"This could be Bill's last summer with us."

"How old is he again?" I asked

"Ninety-seven," responded Nancy. She didn't have to say anything else for us to know that a film reel of memories was running through her mind.

"Do you think Ellen will keep the house and continue to host when Bill passes?" Mike asked as he turned onto I-95.

"Probably not. It's a lot for Ellen to handle on her own." Nancy sighed. The implicit message was clear: *the moments are fleeting, enjoy them while you can.*

"It's a good thing we left so early; the traffic isn't so bad. We're making great—" The adults in the car yelled at me not to jinx it. The drive from Dartmouth to Yardley typically took about five hours, but I was still traumatized from the time we got stuck in bumper-to-bumper traffic for nine long hours. We had learned our lesson since then, leaving at the crack of dawn. This time, we made it back to Yardley in less than five hours, and settled back into our routine.

A few days later, we piled back into the minivan stuffed with beach gear and drove up the coast for a week on the Jersey Shore. Our bright and airy house was steps from the beach, and every morning we piled chairs, towels, boogie boards, umbrellas, a cooler full of sandwiches and seltzer into a beach cart. Pop Pop and Mike hauled it to the water's edge and set up camp, as we plodded along behind them, ready for another day of lazing in the sun. Benji looked forward to his daily frozen treat from the Fudgy Wudgy Man.

Eventually, the tide crept up and the sun dipped towards the horizon, signaling that dinnertime was approaching. A ramshackle bungalow called Mike's (not to be confused with my husband) was our favorite splurge. It wasn't fancy, but the seafood was fresh. Perched in the marina, its weathered shingles were whitened by decades of sun, salt, and sea. The oppressive heat broke as dusk settled in. We joined a long line of hungry patrons that stretched across the parking lot. Eventually, we were seated at one of dozens of sticky wooden picnic tables.

A cheerful server in a purple T-shirt dropped off a bucket of ice for the bottle of wine we'd brought, along with four plastic cups. Another server brought two large trays of steamed clams sitting in pools of butter, garlic, and parsley. We pried open the shells, pulled out the meat, and popped the chewy morsels into our mouths, butter dribbling down our chins. Slices of fresh sourdough, still warm from the oven, sopped up the melted butter. Icy cold white wine washed down the decadence.

I wanted to savor every sweet drop of our vacation, to find solace in the warm folds of this family I'd married into. I longed to find joy in my son's bond with his grandparents, to see the wide grin on my husband's face that rarely appeared back in California. I wanted to let myself belong in this space, with these people.

But beneath my placid smiles and "go with the flow" attitude, anxious tension coiled inside me, ready to snap. Everything felt too stable, too normal, too perfect. I felt as though I was tiptoeing on a glass surface, my body tight with tension, afraid to make any sudden moves. Because deep down, I knew the glass floor would eventually crack.

Family vacations had never been part of my childhood. My parents were immigrants from Korea who prioritized economic survival above all else. My siblings and I learned not to ask for vacations, but I always yearned for them. I longed to be like the white American families on TV who piled into station wagons, sharing funny stories and sing-alongs. Instead, I spent every weekend working the till at my parents' liquor store, where I bagged bottles of Seagrams or Hennessy and handed over loose cigarettes at 9 a.m. to customers who already reeked of booze.

My parents preached that leisure was a waste of time. If I wasn't in school, or doing homework, I had to be working at their liquor store or doing chores around the house. If I dared complain that I was tired, rage would blaze in my mom's or dad's eyes, as they reminded me that THEY were the ones who were tired. THEY were the ones who'd left their lives in Korea to give us a better existence. THEY were the ones who worked 16-hour days to make our lives easy. The only way to gain my parents' approval was by being productive and accomplishing goals.

I carried this persistent drive for productivity with me into adulthood. Empty hours and long stretches of unplanned days did not calm me. Instead of leaning into relaxation, my anxiety and stress spiked. My hands itched for order, writing out a daily schedule and task list for myself, as if perfect symmetry could steady the chaos inside me. Every unproductive moment felt like a glass filling closer and closer to the brim, threatening to spill over. But most days, I gave in, nodding quietly as plans formed around me, letting the glass tip and spill, abandoning the mental list that once dictated my every move.

Beneath my obedient smile, my inner self bristled and strained, rearing its ugly head. Once adorable quirks became nettlesome. My father-in-law is the most loquacious man I have ever met. He loved to engage in philo-sophical discussions and asked a lot of questions. Like their father, Mike and his siblings are outgoing and have strong personalities. But the con-stant chatter and banter became taxing for me. I couldn't understand how everyone in my in-law family could be so pleasant all the time. I tried to keep up, pasting on a smile and waiting for it to feel real, but it all felt so fragile, glass that could shatter at any minute. I swallowed my annoyances.

The problem with bottling up your feelings is that it's only a temporary fix. The glass of my emotions filled steadily, cracks forming under the pressure, and every few days, I could feel it threatening to shatter.

Sometimes I lashed out at my husband, ranting about the *monumental sacrifice* I was making by spending a month with *his* family. Sometimes I threatened to leave. Sometimes I cried or yelled incoherent, obscene nonsense. Mostly, I just locked myself in our room and dashed off angry texts to my girlfriends. After my explosive tantrums, I eased into regret and embarrassment, attempting to repair the damage I had caused.

During our last few days in Pennsylvania, we dipped in and out of the pool, read, and played board games. My husband's stress wrinkles relaxed, and his easy grins appeared more frequently since we were surrounded by his family—his happy place. I, on the other hand, was restless, checking my watch and calendar more frequently. My suitcase was already half-packed, and each unstructured day grated on me like a diamond scratching glass.

Our bedroom upstairs had a view of the backyard, and I watched everyone below sitting in the hot tub and doing cannonballs into the pool. I was so sick of getting wet, drying off, and getting wet again. I was tired of having no control over my time and schedule. I couldn't bear any more time being surrounded with people. I just wanted to be in my own space. Sleep in my own bed. Cook in my own kitchen. Drive my car without asking for permission or providing explanations.

Their laughter carried up to the window and broke my reverie. It suddenly occurred to me that our time together was slipping away. We only had a few days together, and we were in the final stretch. I knew I'd regret not spending more time with my family. Why couldn't I just appreciate having such a wonderful family and the gift of being with them? With so little time left, I should have been cherishing each second, not yearning for an escape.

My routine would always be there, but these moments were fleeting. And I would regret missing out on swimming outside in the middle of a summer afternoon with the people I loved most in the world.

Without hesitation, I ripped my clothes off, rushed into my bikini bottom and pulled on the top. I ran downstairs and joined everyone outside.

Out of nowhere, a fat droplet of rain hit my shoulder, then another and another.

"It's raining?! Should we go inside?"

"There's no thunder or lightning for another few hours," Nancy said. "We'll be okay." My son was the only one in the pool; the others were huddled in the hot tub under an umbrella. The rain was coming down faster, dark speckles on the concrete bleeding into one another until the entire ground was wet.

"Is the water warm?" I called out to Benji over the staccato rhythm of the rain.

"It's like bath water!" he yelled back before dipping underwater.

Instead of easing my way in, inch by inch, I ran to the edge, held my nose, and jumped into the deep end until my feet hit bottom. Every pore shrank, and my body contracted into itself from the cold. The water was not warm, but it was a refreshing relief from the oppressive humidity. I shot up 13 feet to the surface and swam to Benji. I pulled him in for a hug, and he clung to me, a wide smile spreading across his face.

"Don't these raindrops feel like sharp pieces of glass on your skin? It kind of hurts! Let's have a floating contest and see how they feel on our faces! Whoever can stand it longer wins!"

"Okay!" Benji exclaimed. We rolled onto our backs, eyelids shut. Rain pelted my face as I floated. My ears dipped below the surface, drowning out the thrum of rain, the roar of the wind, the flapping umbrellas. The sky hurled a million tiny, jagged pieces of glass into our faces. We shrieked and tolerated the stinging pain as long as we could before laughing and ducking under for cover.

The stress of the last three weeks melted away. All of a sudden, nothing mattered other than being in the pool on a warm summer night in the middle of a storm. If only I had spent less time grousing about the minor inconveniences that felt so big in the moment. If only I dove into the deep end more often.

Taking Measure

JANE MCCAULEY

DUFFEL BAG

I can never decide:

1 pair of underwear per day or half that and do laundry?

Diamox/Antibiotics/Neosporin/Allergy medicine/Band Aids(assorted)/Moleskine/Sunscreen

Chapstick/Eye Drops

Itinerary

Passwords

Travel insurance

Extra assurance for my mother and children.

Zip duffel. Smell of dust.

DOHA AIRPORT

Standing in line to get into the lounge; it's moving slowly

air still and warm

hint of perfume

a crowded room ahead; thankful for potato chips in my backpack.

My mother's worry every time we say goodbye ringing in my head:

"I'll be fine," I always say.

Sixteen hours in the air. Four to go.

Waiting.

KATHMANDU

Almost dusk, mountain peaks puncture the sky.

The sunset, a raucous blast of pink, orange, yellow, then purple

ready to shift to night.

I am tall here. Even taller than some buildings.

The earth rumbles and bricks fall into the street. Eating dinner, I hold
my plate as it rocks back and forth on the table.

People die. Three that I know of.

LUKLA AIRPORT

One guy threw up and another screamed—he thought we'd run into the
side of the mountain.

He must have watched the catalog of crashes on YouTube. Maybe the
other guy drank tap water

or ate street food.

I once argued with an engineer. He asked me how I could get on an
airplane if I don't know how

it works. *I go with the odds*, I said. *And, by the way, fuck off.*

Goats everywhere.

HIKING

Feet hurt; toes crushed. Body creaks, needs oil.

A happy tent. Shuffling sleeping bags, quiet snores, whispered conversation. Dogs barking.

At 15,000 feet, it's snowing.   I wear a hat and gloves in my sleeping bag. I have to pee but hold it.

GOKYO PEAK

An icy 2 a.m.

on the mountain and I see a line of headlamps. We are not first. And we are not last.

Finding footing in the dark.

I force a smile and feel better.

Hours of silence.

Finally, light in the distance, sun rising, we all gasp for air.

Near the top. No. There's another top, and another

(and another).

My feet are clubs of ice, my legs are wood.

Only my upper body has joints.

THE SUMMIT (17,575 feet)

At last. At last!!

Delirious. Headache, barely moving.

I am tired and so damn cold,

I want to go down; *why did I do this?*

This isn't peace.

Only later I realized that

from the top,

I saw my way home.

Marché St. Martin

CIARA O'LAOIRE

I arrived in Paris in September of 2007. A pre-market crash golden moment, I had a job waiting for me. My boyfriend Guillaume had found us an apartment in the 10th arrondissement, Amelie's Paris, one of tiny shops, cafes, canals, and oddballs.

I loved the wooden beams of the apartment ceiling, the weird curve to the kitchen wall where the hallway staircase pushed into the space, the bedroom windows that cranked open so quintessentially over a courtyard and had shutters on the outside. I didn't love the half-wall blocking the light to the living room, but for 800 euros a month and four major metro stops within easy reach, I couldn't have it all!

I discovered the Marché on my first day as a resident of rue du Château d'Eau. Literally across the street from my enormous cobalt blue door was an indoor market, *marché couvert*.

Paris is famous for its markets—flea markets, food markets, markets full of flowers. Les Halles, now north of the city, is nearly a village of its own, but every neighborhood has pop up marchés in the open air several times a week.

Marché St. Martin was atypical since it opened every day but Monday and was indoors. Originally built around 1850, the market was reconstructed in 1880; it feels strongly Haussmann, featuring *pierre de taille* stone facade entrances that are still preserved today despite many renovations.

On my first walk-through, I was overwhelmed by the vivid colors, scents of over-ripe vegetables, and din of chatter from the high ceilings with no premonition that by the end of the year, I'd be a regular. Another year after that, I'd be asked by the cheese man for tips on local apartment hunting!

I had recently spent a summer in northern Ghana, and as I stood in the stone archway of this Parisian space, with lights, running water, ice and more, I was struck by the memory of the markets of Tamale in all their bustle and dust.

It was September, so the last of the summer fruits were still on display: ripe figs, deep red raspberries, and golden Mirabelle plums. Everyone was catching up on August holiday adventures.

"C'était bien le Sud?"

"Vous êtes bronzé!"

I am not a quiet person, but I was nearly church-like in my reveries. Everywhere I turned, there was something beautiful and delicious.

Melons that fit in my hand, not at all the giant cantaloupes I knew from Midwest farmers. Flat fish the size of a dinner plate, eyes nearly following me around in its freshness.

"C'est quoi ça?"

And on to the Butcher counter, land of *lapin,* where it would be nearly a year before I gathered the courage to order by myself. I practiced the phrasing of my order over and over as the line moved forward; palms sweating, like 8th grade math class all over again.

Because I was too afraid to order, I decided that the butcher fancied Guillaume and not me; blaming it on not knowing the French cuts of meat. The vegetable guys were my people, I knew their language—*tomate, chou-fleur, roquette*! They were gentle cabbages of men, speaking softly to their lettuces.

Guillaume believed the fishmonger was my man; I wasn't bothered by the whiff of sea, and he was patient with my linguistic fumbles.

But on to center stage, the fromagerie where the line stretched around both sides of the glass cases. An island in the middle of the *marché*, their stand was set higher up as though they were anointing their customers with cheese from above.

It was there that I learned to wrap cheeses in wax paper, to let them breathe. To give orders by the widths of my fingers. "*Une tranche comme ça si vous plaît?*" Holding my index finger to my middle one.

Mmm, the roquefort, the tome de savoie, the chevre sprinkled with ashes, the absolute funk of the air!

Charles de Gaulle once said, "How can anyone govern a nation that has two hundred and forty-six different types of cheese?"

Based on the boisterous line at the fromagerie, I'd say he was right.

The Italian *traiteur* was ever so tempting, lush with antipasti and home-made pastas. He once said, "You are here all the time, and you never buy from me!" But it was because we couldn't afford his prices.

Once in a while, we succumbed to his allure and bought cannoli. He touched the cream with drops of orange liqueur, the pastry shells lightly coated on the inside by a slick of dark chocolate and finished with a candied orange peel.

No other cannoli has ever come close.

In the years that we frequented the market, the empty spaces were filled by an array of ethnic food purveyors bringing the flavors of French colonies from the Antilles and Morocco, filling the air with spices uncommon in traditional French cooking, fritters of curried fish, towers of couscous.

Today the area has gentrified, and the *marché* has become rather posh. Around 2016, Top Chef France contestants opened a restaurant in the *marché*, which raised its profile.

The Moroccan place is still there, going strong. And as ever, *le marché* offers the essentials: fruits, vegetables, meats, fish and of course, cheese! No meal is complete without *une baguette*, thankfully easily found just down the street—*"pas de panique!"*

The marché was inspiring for me, challenging me to try new things and break out of my grocery store comfort zone of anonymity and engage with Parisians and the language I was so afraid of. I made beautiful pasta salads with rosé marinated chicken tucked in, to be eaten along the canal on a day off. Roast duck with chocolate sauce for a friend's cooking competition, and the freshest of *haricots verts*, which I served crisp, American style, to my horrified French in-laws, who were more familiar with vegetables steamed into submission.

The marché deepened my life-long obsession with food. Allowing me to explore new flavors, embrace seasonality, and sometimes find the pieces to assemble comfort foods when I felt far from home.

Whenever I see thick stalks of white asparagus appear among all the green ones, I think of my *marché*, and of course I buy them, no matter the price. Racing home to poach the stalks gently and bathe them in a warm vinaigrette, I taste memories even when I'm thousands of miles and many years from that first market visit.

Chasing memories on my plate.

Colorado, Here We Come!

MAUREEN SHEA

My sister and I stood optimistically with our thumbs out on the corner of a busy street in Rockville, Maryland. We held a brightly-colored sign containing one word in large letters: COLORADO. By my side was my black and tan German Shepherd, Lupo, and by Lupo was a large, extra-strength black garbage bag containing my sister's belongings. I had a backpack with some clothes, dog food and water, and a shoulder bag with snacks and more water.

We were wearing shorts and T-shirts to accommodate the steamy summer weather and were trying not to be daunted by the poor odds of anyone picking us up to take us to Colorado. We stood to the side of the honking traffic and grungy blacktop, hoping this adventure would be better than our last one, especially with Lupo to protect us.

The breezy, sunny morning seemed like a positive omen of good things to come. Regardless, we had no other choice. No public transportation would allow dogs so, to wish us luck, our friends gave us an ounce of weed, new gym shoes for Reggie, new jeans for me, a $200 donation from my brother, and sent us on our way.

It was 1977, and I had finished my first year of graduate school at Colorado State University in Fort Collins. My parents had sent my 18-year-old sister back to the United States from Río to begin junior college in Maryland. But from the outset, my sister was at a disadvantage. She had come in December, leaving a 100-degree summer in Río to arrive to freezing temperatures in Maryland with few winter clothes and very little money.

She quickly found a bartending job and a basement apartment and struggled to get by in her classes. She couldn't afford books and had never developed good study habits, having barely graduated from high school in Brazil. So, when she called me in March and told me she was flunking every subject, I advised her to drop out before she ruined her academic record.

She also told me that her foreign landlords had enlisted her to be a witness to a fake marriage, to ensure the citizenship of one of their relatives. I was already worried about her so, as soon as my semester ended, I gave up my rental and Lupo and I caught a ride from one of my roommates to Maryland to collect my sister and take her back to Fort Collins.

We had always been close, and we hadn't seen each other in a year, so our reunion in her dingy basement apartment was emotional. But we had no transportation for the return trip, which is how we ended up on the corner of Rockville Pike, hoping someone would pick us up.

We stood there for about an hour, while Lupo sat patiently by my side, happy to be going with us. We admired Regina's new lightweight sneakers, an improvement over the discarded worn-out sandals she had been wearing. We watched a lot of cars go by until finally, a car pulled over and the three of us hopped into the backseat. A young guy our age was driving with his girlfriend in the front. They wanted to know if we were really going to Colorado? When we nodded, they shared the joint they were smoking; we were off to a good start! They took us only a short way, wishing us luck as they left us off at the ramp up the Beltway, where Reggie immediately tried to flag them down. She had left her shoes in their car! But the couple was gone, along with her new shoes, and she would have to do the rest of the trip barefoot. After that, we caught a series of short rides from people going to work until finally, we were dropped off on Route 50 that reportedly went all the way to Colorado.

By then, the sun was beating down, so we had Lupo wait in the shade of some bushes by the highway; he was trained to stay unless called. His dark coat blended in with the bushes although he kept a watchful eye on us, ready to move when we did. Reggie also stood to the side, off the blacktop in her bare feet.

We were picked up numerous times for short rides; the annoying ones were the semi-trucks that would brake for two young women but as soon as we ran up the 500 feet or so to the truck and they saw Lupo, they took off. This happened time and time again until we just shook our heads, pointing at Lupo. One driver didn't see Lupo until Regina and I pulled and pushed him up the ladder to the cab.

He yelled "Don't bring that dog in here!" but it was too late, Lupo had already jumped over the seat onto the driver's cot in the back, thumping his tail happily.

The driver grumbled, "He better not have fleas," and off we went.

He was a balding, elderly guy who groused the whole ride about *the dog*. We were relieved when he let us off at a truck stop after a couple of hours and by then, we were tired, hot, and out of water since we had given most of it to Lupo. We refilled our water in the bathroom, shared our hamburgers with Lupo, and were back on the road within an hour. We walked away from the truck stop until we found a few shade trees and waited.

It was mid-afternoon when a brown sedan pulled over. Two middle-aged men looked out at us and hesitated when they realized Lupo was coming with us. But one got out and put a blanket over the back seat, invited us to throw our things in the trunk, and we began the next stage of our trip.

The driver, a balding, spectacled man named Fred, was quiet but the other one, Steve, was smart, educated and interested in discussing all kinds of philosophical questions. We talked for hours about the meaning of life, U.S. imperialism in Latin America, dogs, economics, and other subjects. I noticed his attention was focused on Reggie, her good looks as usual attracting attention. When the subject changed to drugs, I asked Steve if he had ever smoked pot.

He said he had, although not in a long time. But he would like to try it again, and did I have any on me?

So, I pulled out a joint, and Reggie and I smoked it with him, Fred declining. The mood in the car lightened up considerably, and we laughed at all kinds of goofy things as the car sped on, Fred surpassing the speed limits. Regina, Lupo and I relaxed and enjoyed the ride as we crossed the border from Illinois into Missouri, and much later, Kansas.

Late at night, they pulled into a hotel. We thanked them for the ride, but they insisted on getting us a room, promising that it was only a goodwill gesture with no strings attached, and they would drive us much further the next day since they were going in the same direction. So, since we had had no problems with them so far, we accepted, taking Reggie's trash bag with her belongings and my backpack out of the car with us. Luckily, the motel allowed pets, so they checked us all in, and we went up to our separate rooms,

Reggie and I happy at our good luck. I figured we only had to get through Kansas and after that was Colorado! We fed Lupo and told him to stay; shortly afterwards, we met the guys at the hotel restaurant that was about to close but served us beer and dinner. It was enjoyable, but I was on my guard; Steve, especially, was becoming too friendly with Reggie. Soon after, I stated that we needed to walk Lupo and retire for the night. But when we returned to our room, they were waiting outside the door and asked us to join them in their room for another drink. We refused politely, but they insisted, blocking the door.

"We really need to get to bed," I said, trying to move through them.

"Come on," Steve said, "Just one little drink," as he playfully tried to grab Reggie's hand.

Then Lupo growled at him, low and menacing. "Whoa" Steve exclaimed, backing off. "We were just being friendly."

We were relieved when they left. A short time later, the phone rang; they were getting drunk and demanded we join them, and *don't bring the dog*.

After that, they called every few minutes, becoming more and more insistent, until finally we stopped answering. My sister and I had had a similar experience hitchhiking in South America, but at least the locks on motel doors in the United States were secure! And, we had Lupo!

The next morning, we woke up early, relieved that we had a ride for the next few hours, thinking the guys would have slept off their inebriation by then. But they didn't answer their phone, so we put on our swimsuits and went to check out the pool. Reggie, Lupo and I jumped in, having a grand old time splashing around until the motel janitor saw us and started yelling at us about having a dog in the pool. We laughingly apologized as we got out and hosed Lupo down, changing into dry clothes back in our room, while I dried Lupo with a towel.

We called the guys again; no answer. We asked at the desk and sure enough, they had left early in the morning--taking with them my shoulder bag with my new pants, our ounce of pot and our snacks.

Our spirits sank low for a while; we would have to do the rest of the trip straight and with no food. We felt stupid enough for trusting those guys, and I was especially mad at myself for thinking they would pay for our hotel room with no strings attached. I was the older sister and should have known better!

We discontentedly got back on the road, arguing with each other about whose fault it was, which is how we dealt with stressful situations. So, there we were, refusing rides from semi-truck drivers and getting occasional short rides. We were still in a rotten mood in mid-afternoon when a small, red convertible pulled over and we met Sun, Moon, and Meadow.

The three were sitting in the front, and their back seat was covered with luggage so I thanked them and told them there was no way we could all fit, especially with Lupo.

"On the contrary," they said. "We stopped because we felt sorry for the dog, so we'll make room."

Meadow and Moon got out to move the luggage around, which only left one open spot on the back seat that they assigned to Lupo. Reggie and I were told to climb onto the luggage and hang on. I had serious doubts about this, but with no better options in sight, we all squeezed in, Lupo having the best seat by far. He curled up contentedly.

Our bad mood from earlier forgotten, Reggie and I grinned at each other as we sat on top of suitcases, leaning forward to grab hold of the seatbelts, hanging on awkwardly. We had already noticed how scantily dressed they were; Meadow and Sun were only wearing tiny bathing suits that barely covered their genitals, Moon had on a halter top and bikini bottoms. It turned out that even that flimsy attire bothered them because, as they explained, they were nudists. As a matter of fact, they were heading to their nudist colony outside of Denver, and they hoped we'd go with them. Before we took off, they shared the pipe they were smoking and, for a while, it was a lot of fun.

I wondered about their names, or monikers, but it soon became clear by their interactions that Sun was the leader, Meadow, his apprentice and

Moon, one of Sun's women. They were all beautiful: Sun, a tall, bronzed handsome man with dark hair, expressive eyes and a fit body. Meadow had deep, green eyes along with a muscular, perfect body; they both had one arm around Moon, who sat between them; she was deeply tanned, petite, with a flat abdomen, short brown hair and sparkling, blue eyes. They were vegan, worshipped nature and had sworn an oath to never hurt any being.

It also became evident that this was a patriarchal structure, with Sun calling the shots. I speculated that their names meant that Moon revolved around Sun, probably with other women, and Meadow depended on Sun for sustenance. I suspected, by Sun's glances in the rearview mirror, that he wanted to get us both--but especially my attractive sister-- to their colony--and naked.

Both my sister and I were open to new relationships, but we began to feel uncomfortable at Sun's insistence that we travel with them to their nudist colony. Plus, we were precariously perched partly on top of the luggage in a convertible traveling at top speed through Kansas and had to hang on for dear life.

Happily, Lupo was snug in his corner, dozing off and on but watchful. After we had traveled with them for what seemed like a long time, big drops of rain began spattering on us. Sun pulled over to put up the convertible top and as it came down on top of us, Reggie and I were squashed together like pancakes. With our heads mashed down on our knees, we couldn't even turn our heads to look at each other. We traveled that way through the rain for an hour or so, but we could barely breathe; even laughing at our predicament hurt.

As much as we hated being left out in the rain, we needed to get out before every muscle cramped or we suffocated. Sun didn't want to let us go, and Meadow and Moon added their protests that we should at least let them take Lupo for his own well-being until we came by to get him. But

I was adamant that Lupo stayed with me always and we had to get out, so they made us promise that we would visit their nudist colony. We gave our word and maybe meant it at the time, but we never saw Sun, Moon and Meadow again.

They dropped us off about 300 miles from Denver under some trees by the road. We stretched and the three of us peed behind the trees. After a while, a blue, beat-up pick-up truck driven by a white-haired farmer stopped; he felt sorry for us and the dog in the rain, but he wouldn't let Lupo in the cab, so I snuggled with Lupo in the bed of the truck under a tarp that the farmer handed me, while Reggie got in the front. The tarp, which smelled like hay, kept us dry although the spattering raindrops as we sped down the highway were deafening, and the hard bed was uncomfortable.

I was relieved when the rain stopped, and we emerged from under the tarp and let the wind refresh us. After several hours, the farmer dropped us off about 50 miles from Denver, pointing us to a motel, so we were able to get a room for the night and relax out of the rain. We were ecstatic, only a couple of hours from Fort Collins! Since I had given up my rental there when I left, I had friends we could stay with until we found our own place.

The next morning was a cloudless, sunny day, the air crisp, the sky the deep blue of Colorado, and we had a clear view of the snow-capped Rockies in the distance. Reggie was in awe. I believe that's when she fell in love with Colorado, which she soon made her forever home. At that moment, though, we went down to the motel pool, made sure there was no one around, and jumped in with Lupo. We felt refreshed, happy and relieved that our trip was almost over.

On the final stretch on highway 25, we almost immediately received a ride from a couple traveling to Fort Collins! And then I remembered we left our swimsuits hanging in the motel bathroom. We arrived in Fort Collins with only one pair of shoes, one pair of jeans, no weed, no shoulder bag, no swimsuits, no food, as if we had shed our past as we traveled to begin a new life together.

Rubber Time: Bali, May 1998

EILEEN FITZMAURICE

Josh and I rode the small ferry to the mainland in silence as the rain fell hard over Gili Trawangan. We'd spent the last leg of our 10-day Asian adventure on Gili T, as we'd learned to call it, less than six square miles of pure paradise and the largest of three small islands off the coast of Bali. The incessant sideways rain, the backpack jabbing me in my side, and the crowded boat ripe with the smell of mildew were welcome distractions from my emotional pain. Our relationship was over. I'd been so excited to meet up with my friend Ruth in Asia, I never imagined I'd be leaving with a shattered relationship and a long journey home to sort out the jagged pieces.

I remember the day Ruth called to invite me. "Ei, you have to come visit me in South Korea," she said excitedly. "Or you could meet me in Thailand! A group of us are planning to go in the spring and then travel to Indonesia. You would love it here! We teach for six months, then travel for six."

With every detail she shared, my heart raced with excitement. I loved traveling. After my first international trip to London in high school, I was hooked. In college I was a free spirit, spending a summer in Europe, driving from New Jersey to California with friends one summer, and right after graduation, visiting Guatemala and Alaska. In some ways, I was sorry I hadn't chosen the same path as Ruth after college, but I was comfortable in my career as an editor in a publishing company. Besides, Josh wasn't much of a traveler. As the eldest son in a traditional Italian-American family, he preferred to stay close to home, and to his mom, especially after his dad passed away.

"Ruth, I read an article in the *Times* about companies that offer cheap flights from New York to Asia in exchange for couriering TSA-certified packages," I said. "I'd only be able to take a carry-on with me. But we'll be traveling light anyway and moving from place to place, so that could work." I was talking so fast and could feel my pulse racing at the prospect of traveling again.

With each passing minute, Josh's eyebrows furrowed as he listened intently. When I hung up, he jumped on me. "Eileen, I don't think it's a good idea for you to travel alone to a country you've never been to. And with a friend I've never met. It's not safe. Why don't I come with you?"

My jaw tightened. Everything had to be approved by Josh.

Ruth had moved to South Korea to teach English before Josh and I met. Josh was my coworker's college friend and one night after work in the city, she'd arranged for us to be at the same happy hour. He was cute in an arrogant way, and I was attracted to his confidence. His desire to break into the screenwriting business and his long hair, which he wore slicked back in a ponytail, gave a hint of creative spirit. It turned out to be false confidence, one that masked massive insecurity and soon morphed into jealousy and emotional abuse. Over time, he criticized everything from my outfits to my choice of friends with the illusion of playful teasing. "You're wearing that?" he would ask. "That's great if you want to look like your grandmother." My friends found him charming and entertaining, but my confidence took a hit while we were together.

I was annoyed with him for inviting himself on my adventure and furious with myself for letting him join. Somehow, I always ended up feeling sorry for him. How did he do that? His concern for my safety seemed like a convenient excuse to stay close. When we'd met, he loved my independence but after two years, it bothered him. The more I tried to pull away and get some space, the more he clung to me like a fabric softener sheet stuck to a wool sock. That was Josh—the King of Cling.

I often ended up with jealous boyfriends. In the beginning, their extra attention was flattering and helped fill the void from my lack of self-confidence. But when it transitioned to emotional abuse, I retreated—physically or sometimes just mentally. I'd been checked out of our relationship for the last year, just going through the motions. On the outside, we looked like a happy couple, but my heart wasn't in it. I found ways to sabotage my relationships, so they just slowly fell apart. It was cowardly, but easier than being honest about what I wanted. In my twisted brain, it was emotionally safer to be in a bad relationship than alone. If Josh was the King of Cling, I was the Queen of Sabotage. And Liam, well, he was the sweetest sabotage.

Liam was a friend from Australia Ruth had met on one of her many adventures. They had become close and decided to meet in Thailand for yet another adventure. The four of us traveled around Thailand and Bali together, visiting Buddhist temples and climbing volcanoes. What should've been amazing became awful, with Ruth and Josh constantly butting heads. As they fought, Liam and I bonded. I admired his easygoing personality and how he handled all their constant bickering. I was embarrassed by

Josh's behavior. I found Liam attractive, but it wasn't until we got to Gili T that our connection really grew.

For the last few days of our trip, we took a ferry from Bali across the Lombok Strait to Gili T . Just before, I'd suggested Josh book an overnight biking tour of the Gili Islands. "When will you ever get the chance to do something like this?" I urged. He loved biking, and I wanted to put some space between him and Ruth. Their fighting was causing us to argue, and I needed a break from the drama. *One night alone with my friends,* I thought. *Just one night.*

Surprisingly, he agreed to go. As we parted ways and Josh headed to the meetup point for the bike trip on the other side of the island, I felt my shoulders relax.

That night, Ruth, Liam, and I went to see live music at a bar in town some fellow travelers had recommended. There were two guys playing Beatles songs in English, and I was in my element, singing every word and even harmonizing with them at one point. Liam was staring at me with a huge grin. "Didn't know I could sing, huh?" I smiled back.

"I'm impressed," he said in his cute Australian accent and clinked my beer bottle. "Cheers, Mate."

We stumbled home through the narrow, steamy village streets at 3 a.m., kicking a rock back and forth on the dirt road as we walked. At some point, Liam started howling, his long, tan fingers stretched out on either side of his mouth, his head of auburn curls tilted back. He was tall, almost 6'2", and he looked strong and sexy in the haze of the street lamps. Ruth and I joined in, and the three of us bonded like a pack of wolves in the moonlight. Suddenly, a dog started barking, then another and another. We giggled at the chain reaction with a little pang of guilt at creating a disturbance in the quiet neighborhood.

Sweaty and panting, we made it up the steps to the porch of our bungalow. Liam went inside to get a cold drink and came out with a bowl of ice cubes. I watched as he ran an ice cube up and down his golden arms to cool off. I had to turn away. He was stirring up feelings I'd forgotten were possible after three years with Josh. I stared at the moon illuminating the palm trees when suddenly I felt an ice cube slip down the back of my short black sundress.

I wriggled around, trying to shake the ice from my dress. "You rat!" I screamed, grabbing his wrists. Before we knew it, we were in a full-blown ice fight like two little kids. It was exhilarating!

After a few minutes, Liam held up his hands in surrender. "Okay, okay, you win." All I noticed was his bright, white grin glowing from his tan skin.

Laughing, Ruth walked over and grabbed my hand. "Ei, I am so happy you came to see me and got to meet my friends. I missed you, girl. I just wish you could've come alone."

"Me, too," I agreed. "Sorry about Josh."

She rubbed her fingers along the top of my hand and gasped. "Your skin! It's so freakin' soft!" I laughed. She was drunk. "Liam, feel her skin!"

I tensed at the thought of Liam touching me. Was it a good idea, given the attraction I'd been feeling toward him all night? But it was too late. He ran his hand slowly up and down the inside of my arm, and my whole body tingled, then after a deep sigh, relaxed.

"You're right, Ruth. Definitely the softest skin I've ever felt," he said.

Suddenly, all I saw were the porch lights twinkling a little too brightly as I slowly slid to the floor. Maybe it was all the alcohol or the extreme humidity that I wasn't used to, but I woke up inside on the king-sized bed. Other than a bed surrounded by mosquito netting, the only furnishings in the bungalow were a tiny table, two chairs, and a standing lamp. The upstairs loft had a single bed, which was where Liam was supposed to sleep, leaving the king for me and Ruth. But he was sprawled out beside me.

"Wha...what happened? I guess I passed out." I moaned, holding my pounding head.

"You fainted, love. You were bloody mashed and 'probly' dehydrated. You hit the floor of the deck like a bowling pin."

I laughed and shook my head while cupping the bandage on my elbow. "I'm so embarrassed. I don't even remember."

"No worries. I carried you in and fixed up your arm."

"Thank you." I looked around the room. Ruth was nowhere to be found. "Oh, no. Did I... did we...?" My face throbbed as fire rushed up my cheeks.

"No, no, it's not what you think," he said, matching my pink hue. "We were all pissed as a fart last night. Nobody made it upstairs. I don't think my girlfriend would be too happy if anything had happened. Ruth just left to get breakfast."

As if on cue, the door of the bungalow swung open, and Ruth came barreling in. "Josh is on his way up the hill!"

"Huh? He's on his biking trip. He's coming back later." I rubbed my temples.

"Uh, no, because he's walking up the hill, and he'll be here any minute. I don't think he'll react too well to this!" She made a fast, sweeping motion around the room to indicate the messy bed where Liam and I lay side by side.

I jumped up and made my way outside to the porch just as Josh approached. "Hey, what are you doing here?" I said in a slow, sleepy tone. "What happened to the bike trip?"

"I decided not to go," he said curtly. "Why did Ruth just run in here like a bat out of hell? Did something happen between you and Liam?"

"She probably had to pee. And no, nothing happened," I said, gritting my teeth. *Here he goes again*, I thought.

"I don't believe you. I noticed the way he's been flirting with you the whole time." I cringed. His eyes were on fire.

"I'm not having this conversation here. We've done enough damage on this trip."

I apologized to Ruth and Liam and said my good-byes, then Josh and I walked in silence to our bungalow on the other side of the island. The irony of the name, *Good Vibes Bungalows,* was not lost on either of us after what had transpired. It was the sort of place couples in love would revel in with an outdoor shower and a soft hammock-for-two perfectly arranged between Banyan trees over a tiled patio. I'm not sure we were ever those people.

I climbed up the wooden ladder to a bedroom under the thatched roof. I needed to lay down for a while after all the drama. Suddenly a piercing sound blasted from a loud speaker, followed by a voice speaking loudly in Indonesian. It took me a minute to realize there was a mosque behind the resort, and they were announcing the first call to prayer for the day, *Salah.* It was 6 a.m. and since I was too worked up to rest, I decided to check in with my mom before our long journey home.

"Oh, I'm so glad you called." My mother sounded like she was about to cry. "Are you okay?"

"Yeah, why?" She was always worried, but this time, her tone was especially urgent.

"Because Indonesia is all over the news. There are riots and fires and mobs of people running through the streets."

I looked around at the tranquil village. The only sounds were a chorus of frogs and the clicking of a gecko. "Nope. No riots here."

"Well, be careful and get home safe," she cautioned. " I love you,"

"Love you too, Mom. I'll call you when I land in New York."

The next morning at 8 a.m. we boarded a small boat headed back to the mainland. Josh felt like a stranger sitting beside me. In these last ten days, I'd realized he didn't love me at all. He loved love, and some idea of me he'd conjured in his head of the woman he thought I was. I'd never live up to that image. Also, I didn't love him, a realization that smacked me in the face like heavy rain.

Staring at the shrinking island through the morning mist, I remembered the Indonesian expression I'd learned one day while waiting over an hour for our snorkeling instructor.

"Jam Karet," our guide said, watching my distressed look as I checked my watch. "It means *rubber time*. Everything here is very relaxed, Ma'am. Time is not fixed. It's as malleable as the waves crashing on the beach and the sand that pulls back into the sea. Your time is better spent waiting patiently than wasted in anger."

I thought about all the time I had wasted in this toxic relationship and the time it would take for us to get back to our real lives in the United States and sort this out. Time spent traveling to Indonesia with a germaphobe whose idea of cultural immersion was staying in a five-star hotel and watching a perfectly-choreographed Barong dance with a pack of AARP tourists. Josh feared situations he could not control, and as soon as we got out of his comfort zone, his true self emerged. Or maybe that was the person I had chosen to ignore all along. I craved a more easygoing and open-minded partner who embraced adventure. I wanted a man whose passport was full. Josh had barely left the United States.

We taxied from Padang Bai to the Bali airport in Denpasar. *We're not even out of Indonesia yet*, I thought. *Only 21 more hours to go. Great.*

Little did we know the real struggle was ahead. As it turns out, my mother's worrying was warranted.

We stepped up to the ticket counter to check in for our flight. I was sad to leave this beautiful place but exhausted from all the fighting. I just wanted to get home.

"I'm sorry, but all flights to Jakarta have been temporarily suspended due to unstable activity in the capital."

"Sorry, could you repeat that?" I said, staring blankly at the ticket agent.

"No flights to Jakarta. There is rioting in the capital city," he said patiently.

"But we have connecting flights to Tokyo and New York." My heart pulsed in my chest.

He shrugged. "The American and Australian embassies are being evacuated right now. Those flights have first priority."

I leaned against the pole behind me, scared at the prospect of being trapped in the airport with unknown danger ahead of us. Josh was the only person I had at that moment, and the last person I wanted.

"What are we going to do?" I asked in a shaky voice.

He rifled through his luggage and produced a small white bank envelope. "Give me your passport," he demanded.

"Why?"

He slipped a $20 bill in each of our passports and stepped back up to the counter. "Isn't there anything you can do to get us on a flight?" He winked, then slid both passports across the counter toward the ticket agent, the edge of the green bills slightly visible.

The man sighed and shook his head. Was that a look of pity in his eyes, or disdain because like most Americans, we thought we could buy our way out of a crisis?

"I'll be right back. Wait here," he said as he disappeared behind a closed door with our most important documents.

"Why did you do that?" I implored.

"I saw it in a movie once."

My lips tightened. "Are you serious? This is not a movie, Josh. You just bribed the man. We could get arrested!"

"Oh, stop being so dramatic, Eileen."

"Dramatic? *I'm* dramatic!" He had pushed a button, and there was no turning back now. "Who's the one who didn't want to take a shower because you were afraid of getting a disease? Who's the one who wouldn't go out at night because you thought everyone was going to rob you? Who's the one who felt the need to follow his girlfriend halfway around the world to protect her!" I was shouting and noticed people slowly backing away from us.

Great. I'm making a full-blown scene in the airport. I picked up my oversized backpack from the floor and looked around. The airport was teeming with people desperate to leave. There were no seats, so I walked back to the pole I'd been leaning against and sat on the floor, using my backpack as a cushion. It felt like hours dragged by. All I could do was stare at the door where the man had disappeared with our passports. I prayed he would return with a set of boarding passes.

Josh paced, adding to my fury. I studied his new leather designer bag. Who brings that on an island-hopping trek during Asia's rainy season? Then I looked at my pliable, waterproof pack with reinforced shoulders and straps for a sleeping mat. Our suitcases were as different as our personalities. Opposites attract, right? Josh just had to grow up. He'd eventually give me my space. My biggest mistake was thinking things would ever change. But as the old Mark Twain saying goes, "There's ain't no surer way to find out whether you like people or hate them than to travel with them."

Luckily, Josh's bribe did not result in our arrest, but in two tickets on the next flight to Jakarta. We made it back to New York in icy silence.

Sadly, our relationship wasn't the only thing in shambles that day in Indonesia. We were traveling on the heels of civil unrest, anti-government demonstrations, and an historical event I would be reading about on Wikipedia for years to come: *Jakarta on Fire: The May 1998 Riots and the Indonesian Revolution*. In the end, massive student protests and riots in Jakarta and other major Indonesian cities brought an end to the 32-year Suharto authoritarian regime. I admired the courage of those students to speak out against injustice, to orchestrate the change they felt they deserved. I've tried to do the same in my life. Speaking up about what we want is the only way change and happiness will come. For now, I try my best to embrace the Indonesian idea of *Jam Karet*, waiting patiently, releasing anger about the past, and knowing love will come when it comes.

One Scene, Four Perspectives

CLAIRE NEWMAN

Human

I'm not sure I would have put a fish pond in my backyard had it not come with the house. But perhaps the universe, as it always does, nudged me toward this spot, knowing what I love and need.

A half a century ago, my grandfather built a pond in his backyard, and when I was small, I loved sitting on a large boulder, staring at the tumbling water, and feeding the fish. It was mesmerizing. I made up stories about the fish and wondered what they thought.

Despite floating almost sixty years downstream, and as much as I pretend otherwise, I haven't changed that much. Now, my backyard pond is part of my daily routine.

But, like other things I love, I can take it for granted. At times, I pass the pond, barely noticing it: when I let the dog out in the morning, when I'm taking trash to the alley, when I sweep the leaves off the back steps.

But mostly, I am grateful it is here. It's a haven where I relax, especially when I've been pulled in too many directions, or when my spirit needs rest, and my creativity needs encouragement.

Cool, clear water gently cascades over the flagstone slabs and onto the stones below, creating a hushing white noise. It is not the kind of white noise that blocks echoes of neighborhood children squealing, a car honking blocks away, or Ollie barking as he leaves the house.

But the water's hushed whispers often silence the cacophony in my head, or at least focus it differently. The gurgling harmonizes with chirping birds and rustling leaves, providing a peaceful backdrop for meditation.

Perhaps it's not the sound but the sight of the rushing water that relaxes me, tumbling over rocks and flowing around lily pads, rushing towards the pump at the far end of the pond. It will complete this journey, again and again, never stopping and seemingly ever quickening.

On an overcast day, the serene water creates a darkened mirrored surface, reflecting clouds and shadows of tree branches. When the sun blazes overhead midday, the surface glistens and the waterfall bubbles look like crystals dripping from a chandelier.

A leaf falls down the waterfall, weaves around the lily pads, and enters the catch basket under a small stone slab bridge. I close my eyes and take a deep breath, my body relaxing and my mind quieting. I connect to nature, fish, plants, water, myself.

Stillness. Tranquility.

Even Ollie, who barked after leaving the house, is lulled into peaceful silence by this forty-square-foot space.

Focusing on my breath, my mind is quiet. Until it's not.

While gazing across the pond and staring at the mossy rocks, I see three squirrels chasing each other. Ollie lifts his head, then returns it to the ground without a yap. He's unimpressed and unwilling to let the darting rodents break the spell. I am not as disciplined. I watch the mayhem, and my mind wanders.

Fish

It's usually peaceful here until early evening when the dog begins to bark, and the human makes a shadow. I recognize her and nearly always emerge from my hiding place: under the bridge, below the waterfall rocks, or beneath the lily pads.

Hiding is safest for myself and the others. I had a larger companion here a few years ago. The humans wondered where he went.

"He was just here yesterday. Where did he go?" They asked for a while.

Only I know what happened. It is best to hide. But I'm willing to emerge for her, because from time to time, she throws food flakes in the water, up by the waterfall.

I swim the length of the pond slowly and calmly. But when the food comes, I whip my tail back and forth purposefully, pass the others, and arrive first.

Flakes drop to the water's surface. The scent of dried squid and shrimp meal is strong in my nostrils. My gills flair with excitement.

But I move cautiously before I eat. There is debris on the surface: blossoms from the redbud tree, bits of leaf from the live oak, elm pollen. They all look so alike from below, especially when I'm hungry.

I test the surface layer with my barbels, rejecting anything that is not supper. When I find the flakes, I open my lips, just above the surface, and devour whatever I can find.

Oh, how divine!

The others know to stay out of my way when more than one of us aims for the same bit of food. If they haven't learned this lesson by now,

I remind them by bumping them with my snout or swimming over them. I inhale the feast while my smaller cousins flock to the pond's edge, where the current has distributed bits of fare in the reeds.

Finished, I search for more, still not satiated. I hoist myself partially out of the water and halfway onto lily pads, searching for flakes. I find a few. As the lily pad submerges under my weight, the remaining particles drift away into the current. With an aggressive flip of my tail, I roll off my lily perch and swim to the far end of the pond, waiting for the current of flakes I have set free to float towards me.

Those green barriers help block food from heading downstream too quickly and into the filter, but they crowd the pond and get in the way of my lap swimming. They are large and succulent now. I nibble at the leaf's edge and savor the delicate taste of the plant. I find them more appetizing in August, so I wait until then to munch aggressively.

I dive to the deepest, darkest part of the pond, nearly three feet below the surface. The water is cold. And I am satisfied for now.

Lily Pad

As soon as the air begins to warm, I eagerly plan my journey towards the surface...

As soon as the weather warms? It's Dallas, for God's sake. It's nearly always hot here and getting hotter each year. Ninety-two degrees in February?

"Nothing to worry about," they say. "We are far from the ninety-six-de-gree record, hit back in 1986."

So, let me begin again. This time with more accuracy.

When the thin layer of ice that formed on the pond during the five cold days of winter melts, I strategize my escape from the muck below. Once I leave the water, I stretch towards the sky, then unfurl on the water's surface, a deep green picnic blanket for dragonflies.

With time, my better half surfaces as well. She is fuchsia at the center, then fades to bubble gum pink and eventually turns white at the tips of her petals.

I do my best to insulate her as the fish swim beneath my cloak and carelessly bump our stems. Pumpkin, who lives up to his name, is the worst offender. But I'm certain none of them would harm us purposefully.

I am both the hand that feeds them and the shield that protects them. I conceal the fish from being too obvious a target of any predator from above. I remind them often to hide in my shadows, and they thank me.

However, there was that large white one they called Moonbeam. Perhaps the humans should have named him Icarus. He disregarded my warnings, preferring to bask in the open water to catch the rays of the sun or the moon.

I am strong now, bright and broad. But as the summer progresses, I become thinner and as the fish nibble my pads, I feel the burn of 110-degree weather.

I dread the seasonal affective disorder I develop in the depths of August. The humans are away. With the flowers gone, heartache envelops me, knowing my better half has disappeared until spring.

Then there is the constant chattering of the water. He is continually gushing. I need him. But I don't need to be reminded of what a fantastic job he is doing and how terrible it would be if he went away.

The hotter the weather, the more he squawks, "See how much you need me?" It is too much. He always thinks it's all about him. What a narcissist!

Water

I am invaluable, yet no one appreciates me in this pond. A rock once called me a narcissist. Now, the lily pads are spreading the lies.

Hey, Lily Pad! There's a reason the saying goes, dumb as a rock.

Everyone in the pond claims I'm all over the place, have a misperception of reality and have confused thinking. All of that is pure fabrication! I'm enthusiastic and resolute. Just ask the rock. I've worn him down over time.

And I'm tired of the fish telling me to calm down. I will not be quiet! I was only calm when the pump broke last summer and wasn't replaced for forty-eight hours. Were the fish happy, then? No! And I am certainly not confused. I'm well aware of reality. There is nothing more real than me. Nothing would be here without me. Not the human, not the fish, not the plant.

But just the other day, the damn birds were arguing, claiming they were unclear if all this is true. But I'm clear, at least when the filter does its job, and the human hers.

I'm misunderstood and taken for granted. I am the workhorse that never stops; others can't perceive my burden. I am always awake: rushing down the rocks from two feet above, creating a gentle splash at the waterfall's base, producing a gentle current through and around the lily pads, passing under the bridge, and through the filter to the pump, sending me through a pipe and back to the top of the waterfall to make the journey again.

I am the constant in this pond and on this planet, so it's understandable why the human would stare at me. I would fall in love with myself if I could look at myself in the water the way Narcissus did.

But still, doesn't the human have anything better to do?

Human

The water flows, the plants thrive, the fish swim. I ponder what they are thinking. I close my eyes and take another deep breath. My body relaxes. My mind quiets.

The Dress

BONNIE JESS LOPANE

What had I been thinking? I didn't think I cared about a wedding dress at all. Steve and I had been living together for 13 years and had finally decided to get married. So, what was I doing going to a bridal shop to look for a wedding gown, at 44 years old, and never married?

"Well, here we go," I uttered as we got out of the car on a sun-filled April morning. My twin sister, Barbara, and I strode into the bridal shop lined with racks of gowns around the perimeter of the open floor plan. Glistening chandeliers draped down from the ceiling, creating an atmosphere of an elegant wedding venue.

A middle-aged mother, probably around my age, and two vivacious young bridesmaids relaxed in French armchairs with upholstered pink backs and armrests. The mother's face lit up as her daughter appeared from a fitting room, breathtaking in a spectacular gown with a long train. The girls squealed and jumped up out of their chairs to get a closer look. Tall and slender, in her late 20s I suspected, the bride looked stunning and would look incredible no matter what she wore.

A ripple of excitement pulsed through me. Getting married at 44 felt like a dream I never expected to come true. Barbara and I had shopped for her wedding gown years earlier when we were in our 20s. Now, here we were again. People probably thought I was the mother of a bride, not *the* bride.

Unfortunately, our mom wasn't able to join us. My dad had been diagnosed with esophageal cancer a few weeks earlier, and she didn't want to leave him alone. My dad seemed to be getting weaker. Steve and I were to be married in September, and it worried me to see him looking so frail.

We browsed through the rack of gowns hanging in heavy plastic bags. I was surprised by my own enthusiasm and how much I was enjoying this. I selected three gowns to try on, in hues of beige, ivory and white, one more exquisite than the next.

"Should I be looking at white dresses?" I muttered. I hadn't expected to be wearing a wedding gown at all, let alone a white one symbolic of all the things I was not.

"You should wear whatever color you want," said Barbara. "This is your first marriage!"

My eyes filled with tears.

A friendly salesperson escorted us to a spacious fitting room lined with six floor-length mirrors. The first gown was a soft, lustrous beige satin with dozens of ecru pearl beads decorating the bodice. I glanced in the mirror and couldn't believe how beautiful I felt, like Cinderella.

The attentive saleswoman carried the train as I nervously made my way out of the dressing room. I stepped up onto the pink platform, feeling absolutely elegant and the center of attention, not something I generally aim to be, but I'll never forget the feeling.

"Oh, Bonnie," Barbara exclaimed. "You look beautiful!"

I gazed at myself in the mirror. Yes, this was really me. I had always loved anything elegant and standing there in that dazzling gown made me feel like a princess. The young bride-to-be and her wedding party glanced over admiringly.

Next came the pearl ivory gown, a princess-style A-line made of lace chiffon with flutter sleeves, so when I moved, the air playfully waved the fabric. Perhaps a little too fluttery for a 44-year-old bride. The third dress, and the one I chose, was a beautiful, princess-style silk organza, with a gentle scoop neckline, a sparkling, crystal-embellished bodice, and a chapel-length train flowing to the floor. The lighting in the lovely shop made the crystals sparkle.

As I came out of the fitting room, Barbara gasped.

"Bonnie, that's it," she squealed. "That's your dress!"

I couldn't wait to share the dress with my mom and dad. Barbara snapped photos to show them later.

Barbara, my mother and I returned to the shop in late May for a final fitting. I was excited for my mom to see my dress. Mom and I had found a lovely dress for her to wear at our wedding, a pale blue organza tea-length with tiny crystals adorning the bodice. Of my three married sisters, only my twin sister had worn a wedding gown, as my two older sisters had eloped. My mother was looking forward to our wedding and seeing another of her daughters walk down the aisle, despite the fact that it had taken me a while to get there.

I twirled around on the platform while my sister snapped pictures. I beamed. The dress fit beautifully and made me feel both elegant and confident. Steve and I were in love and finally ready. I couldn't wait to walk down the aisle in it. I was looking forward to the church wedding with our family and friends there to celebrate.

Spring became summer, and my dad was declining before my eyes. He became increasingly frail and slept frequently.

One day, Steve said, "How about we go down to the courthouse and get our marriage license?"

We stopped by my mom and dad's house that afternoon after speaking with Pastor Tim at my church.

"Judy, Don," Steve said. "We would like to get married here on Saturday evening if that would be okay with you."

My mother looked forlornly at my dad lying in his bed.

"We really want to do this," I said, taking my mom's hand.

"Are you sure?" Mom sighed. "What about your wedding?"

"We'll have a church ceremony next spring," I promised.

"That would be very nice," Daddy whispered in a hushed voice.

Steve went to my dad's bedside and took his hand. "Thank you, Don."

I think I saw a tear in both Daddy's and Steve's eyes.

We were married on a warm August evening as the sun began to set. In an emotional turn, I found myself standing at my father's bedside, Steve and I exchanging vows in a moment that was intimate, raw, and profoundly moving. Steve looked more handsome than ever as he stood next to me at my dad's bedside. His love for me and my parents was never more evident.

My mom sat in a chair next to my dad's bed while my sisters, Steve's sister, Gwen, and his aunt, Cindy, gathered around the foot of the bed. My friend, Tina, had brought a small, round cake and champagne, which were set out on the dining room table. We were happy, yet it felt strange to be celebrating with my dad so ill. After the brief ceremony, Steve and I walked outdoors, and my sister took our photo next to my dad's pink roses that grew alongside their house.

Later that evening, I went into my dad's bedroom.

"I didn't know how much that was going to mean to me," he whispered. I knew how important it was for my dad to hear our vows and know that Steve and I were wed in the sight of God.

"Me either, Daddy."

I leaned down to kiss his cheek.

Ten days later, we knew Dad was reaching the end of his life. He lay comfortably in bed, a pale blue sheet covering his thin frame. I sat in a chair at his bedside talking to him, uncertain if he could hear me.

And then, Daddy began to quietly sing the words to "My Bonnie Lies Over the Ocean." Tears welled up in my eyes.

Dad raised his arm and pointed in front of him, as though he was seeing something far away.

"What do you see?" I asked.

A sweet smile crossed his face, a glimmer of light in the evening shadows. He kept pointing upward.

Barbara and Nancy stopped what they were doing.

"Do you see something, Daddy?" Nancy asked.

"What do you see, Daddy?" I echoed, my voice barely above a whisper, wondering what vision was captivating him. Seconds passed without a word.

"You're not going to tell us, are you?" I asked, smiling.

As nightfall approached, we played Daddy's favorite Hawaiian songs. My sisters and I stayed at my parents' home that evening. We were keeping vigil, one of us staying with Dad while the others and Mom took turns getting some rest.

The next morning, Barbara called us into Daddy's bedroom.

"Things are changing," she said, knowing from her experience as a nurse, that our dad's breathing had slowed.

We pulled chairs into the room, so we could all be together. We sat there for what seemed like a long time, though it was probably only a few minutes.

"How long can he hang on this way?" Mommy said worriedly.

"Our nurses at often say that sometimes it helps if you reassure your loved one that everyone is okay, and he can go," I gently suggested.

Turning to my mother, taking her hand, I said," Mom, would it be okay for me to tell Daddy that he can go?"

"Yes," Mommy uttered, holding back tears, as she watched our dad, the man she had shared her life with, slipping slowly away.

I took a breath.

"Daddy, we're all here with you, and we'll be here with Mommy. We'll take care of her for you. It's okay if you need to go...we love you."

Within moments, Daddy took his final breath, passing away peacefully with my mother and me and my sisters by his side.

The next few days and weeks were filled with planning for Dad's memorial service and interment, followed by cancelling the plans we had made for our October wedding. It was bittersweet, yet we felt good that Daddy had been a part of our wedding ceremony.

A few months later, I was enjoying lunch out with my friend, Lauren. She had lost her father earlier that year, so she was a good listening ear, understanding how I felt. I had asked my brother-in-law, Joe, Nancy's husband, to walk me down the aisle when we had our church wedding the following spring.

"I know it will be lovely, it's just so hard to think about my Dad not being there to walk me down the aisle," I shared.

"Just a thought," Lauren said."Would you consider asking your mom to walk you down the aisle?"

I looked across the table at her, speechless.

"I love that idea," I said. "But I don't think my mom would do it."

"Well, maybe not," Lauren replied. "But she just might surprise you."

The next day was a Saturday, and I was at my mom's house to visit with her.

"Mom, you know that I'm looking forward to our wedding in the spring. But it's going to be hard, missing Daddy."

"I know it is," Mommy said. "But he wanted you to have the church wedding. You promised him."

"I know I did, and we will," I said. "But there's one thing I wanted to ask you," I said, stumbling over my words.

"Would you walk me down the aisle?"

"Of course, I would," she said, without a moment's hesitation. "I would be honored."

Months later, with my dad's spirit beside me, I slipped into my beautiful, sparkling white gown once more. My mother walked me down the aisle, radiant in the lovely blue of her dress glistening with sparkles, my dad's boutonniere tucked inside my dress. I felt my mother's love and the support of my family, knowing that even though things hadn't gone as planned, this moment was perfect.

Now, 20 years later, it feels surreal that I use the word 'widow' to describe myself. I still feel like I should be 35 and in my world with Steve. Instead, I'm 66, having found my path to contentment, embracing my next life.

Opening Windows

EILEEN FITZMAURICE

I asked you once if I was a mistake. The youngest of six kids, I figured there had to be an "oops" child among us, and I was curious to know if it was me.

"You were all mistakes!" you said in your characteristic wise-ass humor.

I laughed, knowing you were joking but never getting the answer I wanted, so I kept asking. *Children were meant to be seen, not heard.* I always asked too many questions.

Like many Irish Americans, I have struggled to find my origin story. Hundreds of years of records were destroyed in the Irish Civil War, and my grandparents were gone before I was two, just ghosts in a photograph. Maybe their past was too painful to pass on, but they never spoke about their lives in Ireland, and they never went back. I was desperate to bring their stories to life and know more of my origins, but my attempts at discovering my roots were met with vague details or playful jokes which are the Irish way.

A young boy with a stutter and black curls, smaller than your peers, growing up tough in the South Bronx of the 1930s and '40s, you told me your younger brother was your bodyguard, and no one bothered you when he was around. The Irish were not the favorites in the neighborhood back then. As a child, I would run my tiny finger over the small scar on your back. "I got stabbed," you said. As your thick curls gave way to thinning grays, I realized your outer machismo was armor for your nervous, fragile self.

Yours was a childhood fraught with disruption and trauma, the details so spotty even you could not recall in the journal I found after you died. There was alleged abuse, and your mother's nervous breakdown that sent you away to live with relatives for a while.

That trauma manifested in fears that followed you across the river to New Jersey, to our safe, suburban life. Fear of fire—no burning candles allowed in the house. Fear of crime—no open windows on the first floor, even in the height of spring when rooms stale with cigarette smoke and dog breath were in desperate need of airing-out. As a child, I always wondered why you never liked first-floor fresh air. . Air conditioners were bolted to sills in the summer to prevent them from being removed.

Every Sunday, you walked to the bakery for fresh-baked rolls while Mom—or *Mama,* as you called her—fixed her face and set her hair for church. There would be no communing with Jesus for you.

"I work every day in that god-damn church. Why would I want to spend my day off there?" you said in your best Archie Bunker voice as Mom cringed.

My siblings and I giggled, loving every bit of your rebellion. Your job as head of maintenance for our Catholic school and church was a blessing and a curse. I was never without last-minute spare change for the vending machines but when I got caught talking in school, your office was a little too close.

Sunday mornings, we scrambled to be the chosen one to accompany you on the ten-minute walk through town, past the movie theater and down the hill to the bakery next to the dry cleaners. My turn never came often enough. Returning home, the smell of bacon filled the house as the dog licked the floor where the spatula had dripped hot grease. You always scooped out the gummy middle of the hot rolls, preferring the hard exterior. I loved to steal the balls of dough off your plate, as if I were claiming a part of you, the part I didn't have to share with my siblings, or Mom, or the dog, or the house or your three jobs.

I can still hear your voice after all these years—so melodic, so smooth. The Nat King Cole of St. Ann's Avenue, crooning in the basement of our three-story colonial and listening to your old 78s—Dizzy Gillespie, Vaughn Monroe, or that Louis Prima song we still sing today. You sat for hours, immersed in music and toying with bits of wood and glue as you created miniature masterpieces. You even made a tiny version of our church once.

I marveled at lamp shades made from plastic bottle caps, moveable windows cut from thin slivers of plastic. Each tiny church pew was stained dark brown to match the oak ones we sat in every Sunday; the deep red rug was fashioned from leftover carpet bits. Every nail, screw and scrap a curated treasure.

Sometimes that glue found its way to your weathered blue corduroy slippers, held together tightly in the jaws of the metal vise in the basement, glue drying on the flaps of the soles, to hold them together for one more day. A child of the Depression, frugality was in your DNA. Those slippers had more lives than the neighborhood cat.

Every year, we asked what you wanted for Christmas, and every year you gave the same response: slippers or after-shave. Months after you passed away, I helped Mom go through your tall wooden bureau and found an entire drawer of unopened *Old Spice* bottles. In the closet, there was a stack of shoeboxes filled with blue, corduroy slippers.

I sighed wistfully and wondered if you wanted to keep the gift-giving simple for us, or for you. In your later years, you were easily overwhelmed by choices. The ten-page Cheesecake Factory menu provoked great anxiety.

"What do I want to eat?" you'd ask Mom.

What did you *really* want for Christmas, though? I'll never know. Perhaps your loving family was enough.

Those slippers, protectors from the cold kitchen linoleum where you sat every night after dinner, drinking tea, poring over *Reader's Digest* and reading the jokes aloud—never having to search too far for an audience.

I sat in that same spot at the old wooden table some Saturday afternoons, while Mom chauffeured my siblings to parties and football practice. I tap-tap-tapped on the heavy, black typewriter the best mysteries my nine-year-old brain could conjure as saxophone sounds drifted up from the basement like a smoky jazz club. We connected in our creativity, you and I.

I long to hear your voice again, and I crave the stories of your past for they are my stories, too. The memories you didn't have or chose to forget. The ones I don't have but am determined to find.

I will piece together your story like bits of wood in the basement, like the notes of your songs. Every random anecdote you shared over the years, or bits of truth we learn now from digging, help build the lamp shades and windows in my house.

I'll fill in the gaps with Mom's stories. She has enough memory for both of you.

And I sit here writing with Mia by my side, your little Muffin, the last of your grandchildren, the one whose little hand you barely got a chance to hold. Did you hold your father's hand before he passed? You were not supposed to leave until all your stories were told.

But Mia will know. I will build this house for her, piece by piece, and I will open all the windows.

Perfect Wasn't in the Moment

JESSICA MONTAGUE

I planned my West Coast wedding while working as a clinical social worker in New York City visiting families in their homes. Riding the subway to my clients, I thumbed through *The Wedding Book: An Expert's Guide to Planning Your Perfect Day—Your Way* by Mindy Weiss. I was in love and fantasizing about my "perfect day," thinking its perfection symbolized whether I'd have a blissful, painless life ahead.

I followed Mindy's suggestions, nailing chapters 1-6. I booked a men's club called the Family Farm 20 minutes south of San Francisco for the wedding. Impossibly tall redwoods surrounded a worn outdoor stage, with rows of wooden benches for guests to watch the ceremony.

While my soon-to-be husband was on his way to mapping the entire redwood range, those incredibly tall trees were important to both of us—my husband was so passionate about research and conservation that we would eventually move into the thick of the forests.

These glorious old trees had been a fixture in my childhood, too. As a kid, I did cartwheels under a giant tree outside my elementary school, Redwood Heights. I wanted to say our wedding vows in a cathedral of old-growth that stood testament to longevity and perseverance, qualities I wanted for my marriage.

After the ceremony, we had cocktails on a cobblestone patio draped with lights under a canopy of branches and leaves. We ate dinner in a grassy meadow. My friends said it was "so tasteful, well-thought-out, beautiful." My parents' friends suggested I become a wedding planner.

But for all of my precise planning, the wedding weekend didn't go exactly as planned—since my grandmother died the day before the wedding.

This wasn't in the book, Mindy.

There is nothing like death to cast aside the most detailed plans. Or maybe death reminds you that life is for the living, and living is never perfect. Perfection may even oppose the human condition.

As an adjective, perfect means "having all the required or desirable elements, qualities, or characteristics; as good as it is possible to be; absolute; complete."

The word doesn't gel with my experience of being a human, which is messy and complex. My heart flutters when I want to be calm. I need to use the bathroom at inopportune times. I misplace keys, forget to respond to emails, stay up too late. I yell, cry, love, and hate—sometimes on the same day!

Being human is having the audacity to try pulling off a large-scale, life-changing formal event and thinking you can make it perfect.

As a verb, perfect means to make "something completely free from faults or defects, or as close to such a condition as possible." From that perspective, perfection isn't fun! Going for perfection is striving for what isn't possible. Save perfection for bridges and brain surgery. Day-to-day human life demands freedom, tolerance, and acceptance.

I bought into a notion of perfection, hoping it would protect me from pain. But trying for perfection only blocked me from feeling and being with what WAS.

***

The bridal suite was set up in a rickety cabin. Against wooden beams, dusty floors, and by the light of a hanging bulb, I smoothed powder over my cheeks among my six best friends, all donning flowy cobalt blue dresses. I practiced my vows while sipping champagne.

John, I promise to be your constant friend and faithful partner, to honor your independent self, and to cherish your uniqueness. I will love you as you are and strive to be sensitive to your needs.

My slim wedding body—I'd lost four pounds I didn't need to lose in the months prior—fit into ruched, off-white, raw silk secured by little buttons. In the dress, I felt secure and confident. It helped contain the flurry of feelings inside me like glitter in a jar of water.

"Relax; you're doing great. You've got this," the photographer cooed as she snapped pictures of me alone.

The photographs turned out terrible, though they revealed a truth, a different picture of perfect: Sitting with what is true, what is real, not a fairytale bride on a fantasy day. My shoulders clenched, my eyes stared out at the trees, I half-smiled and held a bouquet of cream-colored calla lilies.

Inside, I felt lonely. I wanted my mom. Sadness draped on me like a weighted blanket. My heart was heavy, my stomach spinning, while I stood like a statue veiled by professional brush strokes and a custom-fitted dress.

Nonna always had bad timing, saying inappropriate things to waitstaff, blurting out an apt but controversial statement among strangers, telling us it was great when we visited and great when we left, and now dying the day before my wedding.

Death and life share some common traits. They upend perfect plans. Normally, in stressful situations, I cope by not burdening anyone, just keeping it all inside.

So I didn't turn to my mother, my aunts, or my brother because they were struggling, too. I realize now that I wanted my mom available to me that weekend, as she must have wanted her mom. I was 33, starting my own family. My mom was 63, watching her daughter get married, mourning the loss of her mother, pulled between generations.

Despite all of this, the wedding was, in fact, wonderful. Mid-afternoon light faded into a warm night with live music, juicy steaks, and the 165 people I loved most gathered together. Our Scottish officiant recited a poem that moved people to tears. Three deer appeared during the ceremony. We danced to the music of a band called The Cheeseballs.

I got through it by holding John's hands as we exchanged vows. *All* of my family showed up, and there were a lot of them who were mourning like I was. My brother said conversations during cocktail hour were deeper and more meaningful than at any wedding he'd attended because people were talking about real stuff—the pain of loss and the hope that comes with enduring love.

My uncle tapped my elbow. "Jess, go on your honeymoon," he said. "Don't stay for the funeral; celebrate your marriage."

My friends toasted me and my husband, and we danced as we had in college: arms up, booties shaking, making fun of each other, and singing to ACDC's "You Shook Me All Night Long" and anything by Snoop Dogg.

My aunts and my mom's friends interpreted the late afternoon sunlight as my Nonna's spirit shining on us. My husband was convinced that the three deer represented our future family.

Nonna died the morning of my rehearsal dinner. That night, my mother had planned to give a speech. She began by saying, "It's the cycle of life," but could not go on. Tears rolled down her cheeks. I walked over and hugged her. The photographer snapped a picture of our embrace, and it's one of my favorites. My eyes are closed, and my head rests on her shoulder. Our arms wrapped around each other as if we were holding each other up.

We probably were.

Digging to China

SUSAN P. EPSTEIN

When the sun went behind the rain clouds, we scurried up the beach to the stone wall and buried ourselves up to our necks in the warm sand to wait for the sun to peek out.

I grew up in New London, Connecticut, on the Long Island Sound, where summer days stretched forever with Ringolevio, kick ball and bike riding until streetlights came on and we all went home, dirty and exhausted. Our days ended with faces washed and teeth brushed, reading bedtime stories and then falling into the best kind of sleep only tired children can have. Those nights carried the low, mournful call of foghorns, their echoes rising and falling like a lullaby.

When my best friend Rhonda slept over, she would always ask, wide-eyed in the darkness, "How do you sleep with that noise?" The low roll of the foghorns from the Sound were as steady and unrelenting as the tide. I would smile, and say, "What noise?"

I still live in the same town, and last weekend, my brother visited for my mom's 97th birthday. He asked, "Did you hear that?"

He'd been away for more than forty years; I still don't hear the foghorns. They are part of the night, as natural as rustling leaves or the faint hum of distant ocean waves. Their call is woven into my days.

Just a few blocks from my childhood home stands the New London Harbor Lighthouse, a timeless figure etched against the sky. Built in 1801, it rises a solemn ninety feet, weathered stone bearing witness to countless tides and tempests. At the end of a stretch of private beaches, it keeps watch, steadfast and solitary, a keeper of secrets from a quieter time.

This lighthouse was among the first in America with a flashing light, its rhythm dictated by a revolving eclipser: three seconds on, three seconds off. The pattern ensured it could never be mistaken for the steady glimmer of nearby farm lights, a small triumph of ingenuity over the vast, shifting dark.

Beaches stretch along the shore, bordered by a mile-long stone wall that seemed to hold the world together like a thread of quiet intention, marking the edge of land and sea, human touch and nature's endless expanse. During the day, mothers threw beach chairs, umbrellas and toys over the top of the wall to make the carrying easier.

In the 1960s and 1970s, in darkness, the wall transformed from a gateway to children's play to a destination where teenagers gathered to smoke pot, drink Boone's Farm apple wine and lose their virginity. Anyone who grew up in New London can tell the secrets of the wall.

For me, the beaches symbolized a different kind of magic. When I was a child, our family belonged to a private beach, a place claimed by Mrs. Sacchi, a stout, first-generation Italian woman with a crown of curly gray hair and skin worn to leather by the sun. She was as much a fixture on that beach as the endless waves. Membership to that beach meant access to a white-washed, weathered storage shed filled with folding chairs and umbrellas, an outdoor shower that dribbled icy water, and two cramped, cold, damp bathroom stalls—modest luxuries that somehow made the beach feel like a second home.

Mrs. Sacchi reigned from an orange and white aluminum chair under a matching umbrella. With the stateliness of royalty, her reign was marked by a tin pail brimming with quarters—accumulated 50-cent guest fees. The pail hung from her chair like a badge of her authority, jingling softly in the breeze. Once, she handed me one shiny coin, for no reason at all-its surface warm from the sun. Our beach was full of gifts and treasures.

Because we couldn't wait to get there each afternoon, we'd hurriedly eat peanut butter and jelly or tuna fish sandwiches on Arnold white bread, crusts removed. My cousins were lucky enough to have Wonder Bread, which we squashed between our fingers into pill-sized pieces and practiced swallowing them whole. My mom refused to buy it, saying it wasn't healthy. When we visited our cousins before going to their private beach half a mile down the road, I ate as many Wonder Bread slices as I could .

It was never a problem for my mom to round us up. We'd quickly change into swimsuits and flip flops and load our pails and shovels into the back of the car. Mom drove us down the hill and around the corner—even though it was a mere five-minute walk to the beach. Mom sported giant Jackie O sunglasses. At the beach, she quickly claimed her spot, grabbing the umbrella by the throat, positioning her tanned legs in an almost-split, and rocking it to get the pole deep enough into the sand so it wouldn't blow away or hit one of us in the head. We dropped our toys and ran to the edge of the water to cool off.

Once seated, mom never stopped talking and laughing the entire afternoon, all while keeping a protective eye on us. The moms operated like a unit—if one looked away, there was always another on the lookout for a child who might drown. With no lifeguards around, they took their unspoken, shared responsibility seriously. Although our mother never swam with us—she almost drowned as a child and was afraid of the water—she arranged for another mom, Mrs. Wickman, to teach us how. Mrs. Wickman had grown up in Far Rockaway, New York, and was an avid swimmer. She had five children my age and younger whom she taught to be skilled swimmers.

Some years later, I overheard hushed conversations amongst my parents and their close friends that Mrs. Wickman left her husband for their au pair and ran off to live in California, leaving her five kids behind. Everyone was shocked.

When my brother, Matthew, and I weren't swimming, we wandered the beach collecting sea glass in greens, pinks, and blues. We dug up seashells that sparkled in the sun, placing big, barnacle-covered conch shells to our ears to listen to the ocean singing. We hunted hermit crabs, minnows, and snails, but always set them free before we left the beach.

I was especially fascinated by the hundreds of clear jellyfish that we called "moon jellies." Wiggly like Jell-o, we gathered them in our pails and poked and played with them. There was another type of jellyfish not to be played with—bright red man o' war with the longest, ugliest tentacles . We called them "the stinging kind." If any of us saw one in the water, we swam as fast as we could to avoid being stung. But even if we were, we had nothing to fear as every mom—except mine—kept a jar of meat tenderizer in her beach bag. The moms swore that a sprinkle on a sting would immediately cure you. My mom, who was a nurse, thought it was nonsense and instead applied ice to our stings to lessen the swelling and pain. Later on, in researching the meat tenderizer cure, I read that jellyfish venom is protein-based and a specific enzyme in meat tenderizer breaks down those proteins, decreasing the itching and burning.

When we weren't swimming or hunting sea life, we built elaborate sand castles that grew out of our memories of pictures in Grimms' *Fairy Tales* .

We built forts and villages using sticks for flagpoles and flags made of green and red algae, drizzling wet sand over spiral mounds to gave the castles a gothic flair. We dug moats deeply hollowed out of the wet sand circling the castle. We made up stories about princes and princesses and the bad ogres who wanted to get them. Passing by, adults asked, "Are you digging all the way to China?" I had no idea what they meant, but always smiled and said, "Yes!" Years later, when I was a college student studying in Barcelona, I saw Gaudí's Basílica dela Sagrada Família, and I remembered our early sand castles, imagining the artist as a child creating castles on the beach like I had.

On beach days, by mid-afternoon, like a flock of hungry sparrows, we kids would appear from all corners of the beach, summoned by the unmistakable jingle of the Good Humor truck. Monday through Friday, my mom gave each of us 15 cents—just enough for a simple orange or red popsicle, the kind that left sticky trails of bright color on our lips and fingers. We'd yell, "Stick out your tongue!" and then reply, "It's purple! Ha! Ha! Ha!"

Weekends were special. When my dad joined us, he handed out whole quarters opening up a world of possibilities. With a quarter, we could get the crown jewel of the ice cream truck: the chocolate chip candy bar—a luscious chocolate bar cocooned in vanilla ice cream, wrapped in a crunchy, chocolate chip coating.

The hot sun turned every bite into a race. It melted the treats faster than we could eat. By the time we finished, we were sticky disasters, chocolate and vanilla running from our hands to our elbows and smeared across our faces.

After ice cream, Matthew and I and our friends, Ricky and Cathy, gathered under Mrs. Sacchi's umbrella, a throne of calm in the middle of our chaos. Sitting cross-legged in the warm sand, we dropped our popsicle sticks into a bucket of water she'd left out in the sun. There was something mesmerizing about watching those sticks bob and soak, waiting for the moment they turned soft and pliable. When they were ready, Mrs. Sacchi worked her magic, weaving the softened sticks into miniature rafts with practiced fingers.

She handed them back to us, her creations simple yet extraordinary. We ran to the water's edge, our rafts cradled in our hands, and set them adrift in the gentle surf. The hours slipped away as we followed their journeys, wading knee-deep and imagining far-off adventures like the pirate movies I loved watching .

Nothing could interfere with the idyllic unfolding of those days. They were slow and sunlit, perfectly stitched together, held in place by the rhythms of the beach.

For the sake of my own timeline, later that summer or the next my parents gave me a little turtle and I named her "Mrs. Sacchi." She came with a small plastic tray that had a little swimming pool for the turtle to bathe in. Positioned next to the pool was an emerald-green umbrella. We kept her in the living room on the side table next to the sofa. Within a few days, she ran away. I cried unconsolably when she left.

Around the same time, my brother was given a goldfish in a small glass bowl. One morning, when we woke up, we saw that "Goldie" had jumped out of her bowl. Her body lay stiff and lifeless on the dresser. As we screamed and cried, my dad flushed her down the toilet. Over the years, we rescued baby birds whose nests had fallen out of trees in our yard, only to bury them in the backyard in Stride Rite cardboard shoe boxes under a maple tree.

Years later at college, I had a brief urge to become an archaeologist. I felt the pull to dig and uncover the past. In my freshman year, I took an introduction to archaeology class. The professor, a man not much older than me, with long blond hair and wire-rimmed glasses which continually slid down his nose, spent the entire thirteen-week semester discussing soil stains. This was not the romantic, mysterious career I had imagined. I quickly lost interest, switching my major to psychology.

I began to dig in another way—into my own psyche. I wanted to understand why certain subjects had been avoided like talking about death and lesbians. I realize it was my parents' need to protect us, but in doing so, they removed the ability for us to process and move through loss which is part of the circle of life. I had been burying every loss I had experienced. This created a deep fear in me—like looking over my shoulder, wondering, "When would the next bad thing happen?"

Loss and death continued to appear without explanation. Dog losses, Relationship breakups. Actual deaths, of my grandparents, my sister-in-law Deanne at age 25, my best friend Vicki at 35 and two of my husband's best friends at 35 and 42.

When we were young, my father told us that he lost his father of a sudden heart attack when he was 11. When that happened, my grandmother packed up their house and moved his family in with relatives in a different city. My father attended a different school and every morning for one year, he had to accompany his grandfather to synagogue to say Kaddish in memory of his late father. They never talked about the death, the move or why my grandmother suddenly had to go to work seven days a week in the family store. Nor did they discuss why my dad was expected to work there every day after school and all summer long. The sudden change hurt him deeply and rendered him unable to speak to me about my own experiences with loss and death.

As an adult, I returned to New London with my husband, and we bought a house a few blocks from my childhood beach. We joined one of the private beaches along that same strip of shoreline, and I became the mom, prepping dinner in the mornings and spending my days watching my son and daughter play in the sand, collect sea glass, build castles, and learn to swim.

Thirty years have passed and as I walk along that same beach today, I imagine Mrs. Sacchi sitting in her chair looking out at sailboats and the occasional submarine. I pick up a conch shell and press it to my ear, listening to the ocean waves crashing on the beach. The sun sets, and the sand is cool between my toes. I am flooded with images of children, tanned and sandy, eyes wild with curiosity. I move to the edge, that place where the water meets the beach, and play tag with the tide—running back and forth, screaming and laughing, not letting the water touch my sandy feet, as if it might keep me innocent and free from the harsh realities of life.

When I tire of the game, I pick up a shovel and get to work, intent on digging all the way to China with an unencumbered sense of possibility—reminding me that no matter what has been lost or left unspoken, there is still a willingness to explore wherever my dreams and desires take me.

Surviving

KATE ROSENBLUM

Green shoots push through skeletal leaves of last fall, leaving small clumps of soil tumbled to the side. They do not worry about "what ifs," and, defying predictions of frost, their bulbs underground draw strength from warming soil.

I, too, am emerging. Two years since diagnosis, and the unfolding of scans, biopsies, infusions, radiation, and surgeries now behind me, I am faced with the possibility that I might be well.

When first diagnosed, I was gifted a bracelet from a friend whose mother survived breast cancer. Small pink round stone beads, bound by elastic thread, framed little white cubes with the letters: s-t-r-e-n-g-t-h.

"It helped my mother, and now you should have it," she said.

The bracelet stretched around my hand and fit comfortably at my wrist. For weeks I wore it day and night, in bed, or on the crackly-paper-covered exam table in that awkward patient gown. Yet with each passing day, the bracelet fit less. Not in size. No, the elastic band remained 'just right.' But rather than inspiring strength, the black letters almost seemed to mock me: Be strong! Be strong! Be strong!

Strength was the little engine that could. But this is not what I felt.

Instead, with fear, nausea, and exhaustion, I was emotionally bare as my head. "Strength" hearkened admonishments to "kick cancer's butt," a battle with winners and losers. Vulnerable and raw, and with treatment stretching ahead, I could only think about my next step. I needed a new word, a mantra, a guide, chosen for myself.

Now on my wrist, tiny hard grey-blue stones and ten white cubes: d-e-t-e-r-m-i-n-e-d.

Despite hope, another frost arrives. Small shoots exposed, their tips turn gray, and the single yellow blossom, heavy with frost, bends towards earth. Determined, it will stand again, petals less firm and worn, yet surviving.

published previously on breastcancer.org

Good Enough

MerriLee Anderson

I came home to wisps of white paper blowing through the screened-in porch like feathers in a chicken coop. Rosie, the rescue puppy, was sitting on haunches with head bowed and tail wagging sheepishly, white exclamation points in the black spots of her scruffy fur.

The trail of paper led from the porch, through the dog door, to the living room floor, to the black leather cover of my grandmother's Bible, her name in gold on the lower corner.

The hot, heavy feeling of "not good enough" seeped in as I remembered that grandmother. The one who pat the piano bench beside her and fed me the magic words of salvation so that my Daddy could lean me back in the water behind the sliding stained glass windows above the choir loft.

I remembered that warm feeling of belonging as I was baptized by my father, who was baptized by his father. The feeling of connection to something bigger that made me bigger.

I imagined her now, head shaking as she looked at me with stern lips and narrowing eyes. Seeing a sinful woman who plays cards, drinks wine, laughs loudly, dances, married a woman, and let her black leather Bible be shredded.

The feeling of not good enough snuck in quickly like an intruder who has a key to your home. It lodged in my heart and began taking stock of my inadequacies. It made me feel small and quiet.

My grandparents were Baptist in a way that bored me and made me feel like breaking rules. Visits to Pana, Illinois meant no cards, no TV, no swimsuits, no dancing, and no pipe-smoking for my father. Everything in me wanted to join the neighborhood kids at the pool, showing them my flips off the diving board and my handstands in the shallow end.

I wanted to whip out my deck of cards and play solitaire. I wanted to listen to loud music and watch the Jetsons on TV.

Evenings in Pana ended with a family Bible study, during which my older sister would pinch my thigh and cross her eyes, making me shake and giggle until I was sent to the basement where I sat with the heavy feeling of "not good enough" until the prayers were over.

Oddly, the one game my grandparents allowed was "Sorry!" I loved shuffling the cards of the Sorry deck using the overhand bridge shuffle I had perfected during long summer days between second and third grade back in Texas.

One afternoon on the steamy front porch, my grandmother took note of my talent and asked where I learned to shuffle. I pointed to my older sister, so she could have her own moment of "not good enough" as my grandmother stared through her with pursed lips.

When our family of five climbed into our Pontiac Bonneville to head home, I remember the giddiness of escape. Three blocks away, my father pulled his pipe out of the glovebox, my sisters pored through their *Seventeen* magazines, my mother read her who-dunnit, and I shuffled my playing cards. All of us ready to return home, where being a Baptist wasn't so hard.

My father wore the feeling of "not good enough" like heavy shoes. He was a charismatic preacher with a baritone voice and a strict rule to never preach longer than fifteen minutes. When he stepped away from the pulpit, there was a quiet in the sanctuary and a feeling of "more, more, more!"

He needed love and appreciation from everyone and was deeply hurt when rejected. If someone left our church for another church, he would tear up and look at the ground as he walked.

He had the power to move people to laughter or tears, and he used it freely. My mother fed his ego with proclamations of his exceptional talents and disdain for anyone who did not agree. I learned from an early age how to feed his ego to keep him strong and me loved. My mother, sisters, and I rotated around him like moons to Jupiter.

One Christmas card photo has him seated in a chair with my mother behind him, hand on his shoulder and the three daughters kneeling and squatting around him in prim dresses. Looking closely at the photo, one can see all eyes adoringly on my father except for me, the youngest, whose face is pointed in my father's direction but eyes are on the photographer.

On the way home from Pana, we spent a few nights at the other grandfather's house perched high on a cliff above the Arkansas White River. This grandfather wore Sears and Roebuck coveralls in khaki or dusty blue, smoked cigars, and drove so fast down Arkansas back roads that red dirt flew like a tornado around his Cadillac.

His wrinkled face and yellow-toothed grin gave hints of the handsome young man he had been. I bounded through his property like a colt let loose from a stable. I once followed a gopher's trail through the sandy yard to the edge of the grass under the balcony to find a copperhead curled up with tongue lashing, ready to strike. I yelled to my grandfather, who grabbed his rifle, took aim from the balcony, and killed the snake with one bullet.

He then lumbered down the steps, hung the dead six-foot snake on his gun, and swung it in front of my face, grinning as he watched my awe.

Later in the evening his eyes turned squinty and mean as he leaned forward, raised up from his chair slightly, pointed his finger in my face and called me stupid for playing an errant domino. Protector or enemy?

My confusion about this grandfather remained with me for years until I pieced together collected stories. One story I heard several times was of him driving beside my then teenage mother as she walked home from a movie theater, him yelling insults, her crying and fearful. I later learned from an aunt that my mother's mother often had bruises on her face and that her bright personality faded during her years married to my grandfather.

As an adult, I found multiple Dallas area addresses for this grandmother in the months following their divorce, making me imagine her running away from him.

My mother's feeling of "not good enough" was deep rooted into her soul. She worked hard to cover her shame by trying to be perfect. She dressed impeccably, first in clothes she sewed with patterns out of the Vogue catalog, then in clothes she bought at Frost Brothers Department Store. She vacuumed the green shag carpet every morning and never walked out the door if a single dirty dish was on the kitchen countertop.

Despite her best efforts, she still wore her "not good enough" like an apology note pinned to her chest: "Dear World, Please forgive me for being here. Sincerely, Mrs. Donald L.Anderson".

She offered apologies reflexively—"I'm sorry"—when someone ran into her. "I'm sorry," when my father bumped her hand as she served him coffee. "I'm sorry," when she had a stain on her blouse.

Interwoven through all the judgement and insecurities that ran through my family's DNA was also a thick thread of humor. My father's witticisms, delivered with sparkling blue eyes and a lopsided grin, kept us all laughing at ourselves and the world. It was never just chilly outside; it was, "cold as a polar bear's bottom." His friend was not just sad, he was, "so low, he had to reach up to put his socks on."

My mother's loud laughter made everyone's shoulders relax and faces break into a grin as they looked in her direction. Momma's frequent malapropisms such as, "You can't pull the sheep over my eyes!" or "That cowboy in the store was like a horse out of water!" would send Dad into head shaking, then eye rubbing, then chuckling, before he laughed in a way that reminded us she was his joy. Her ability to respond to her own foibles with an unapologetic laugh showed me how she survived her, "not good enough." Humor was the balm for all of us.

After Rosie's attack on my Grandmother's King James Version, my wife Jill and I wandered through the screened-in porch, picking Bible verses off furniture. Weeks later, we still found scripture clinging to blades of grass in the back yard. With each find, we giggled as we shared abbreviated nuggets of wisdom or threats of damnation with each other.

"Better is a poor and wise child than an old..."

"Again, if two lie together then they have heat, but..."

"The eyes of the wicked shall fail"..."Blessed are the peacemakers."

Finding the torn pieces of verses was reminiscent of the way I read the Bible as a college student. On a "not good enough" day at Baylor University, I sometimes grabbed my green hardback Living Bible that was written without the "haths" and "thees" so that a regular person could understand it.

As a lazy Bible student, I would flip through the pages then close my eyes while my finger pointed to a verse. After reading the verse, I would decide if that particular message was the one for me or if I should reflip. While picking tissue paper off grass blades, I found myself hoping for the same kind of inspiration.

Jill and I have stacks of Bibles in our home. Bibles we were given as children. Bibles with names of parents and grandparents on the cover. Bibles with our names on the cover. Each Bible offering varying versions of scripture as well as the memory of a person.

We often pare down belongings, but it is difficult to know what to do with those stacks of Bibles. The worn covers and underlined verses seem like a connection to the souls of our dead relatives.

While I don't have a Bible that belonged to my mean grandfather, I do know that his father was a Baptist preacher who held tight to a Bible and was a comfort to my mother. While Jill does not come from a family of preachers, her grandparents also carried Bibles and attended church. The Bibles represent what was sacred to the people who brought us to this place. We feel stuck with the Bibles like I feel stuck in my heritage; it's there and I don't want to change it. I just don't know what to do with it.

Jill and I attend a church where folks don't typically carry a leather-bound Bible with their name on it to worship, but Bibles are present and ready in the pews. Thankfully, the wise leaders of our church community do not flip through the Bible and point to verses that are convenient for them. We read the Bible as something that needs to be understood through the lens of culture, both when it was written and today.

Jill and I were married in the church courtyard, the first gay wedding at the church. Our female pastor read scripture, reminding us how to love one another and the world.

While I am "Sorry!" I left my grandmother's Bible on a low shelf within reach of a curious puppy, I am relieved to be free of her interpretation of the words within the sacred text. I am appreciative of wise voices that led me to understand the Bible in ways that allow for more love and less violence, more grace and less judgment, more joy and less drudgery.

And maybe that reading of the Bible, along with a good dose of humor, has allowed me to feel "good enough" more days than not.

Awe in Big and Small

KATE ROSENBLUM

I was born by the sea under the canopy of the grand coastal Redwoods. In my earliest years, my father, a marine biologist, took us often to these shores, the morning still dark as we claimed the lowest tide, wading into the salty, dark waters of Northern California.

Up to our waist in swirling, foamy, noisy ocean, traveling between rocks in our raggedy, tide-pooling sneakers, heavy water-logged blue jeans covered and protected our legs from sharp edges as we traversed the seascape searching for sea urchins and nudibranchs. Wading through seaweed, holding onto slippery rocks, even then I was aware of my smallness in this vast water-verse.

We flirted with danger as the tide thundered to shore, and I can still hear the sound of my mother's voice calling us to return to camp for breakfast. We sat together at the wooden table and ate eggs cooked on a Coleman by the roar of the waves, salt in us and on us as we dried and ate and laughed and played.

I always wondered at the magnitude of the ocean, and at the same time, the awe of a universe contained within a small pool, nestled in the rocks—crabs, mulitcolored iridescent seaweeds, swaying sea grass, colorful pebbles, tunicates plastered on rock, barnacles similarly glued, hiding their gentle, swaying parts in their calcified and dangerously sharp exterior.

Small creatures finding place in a water-verse of their own, traveling among rocks, through grasses, waves crashing all around.

I find these repetitions in nature to be so alluring. All around, everything on a grand scale repeats in smaller places.

My son and I delight in watching, and re-watching, the "Cosmos" series together. Neil DeGrasse Tyson takes us on the "ship of imagination" as he shows that almost all is space.

Our galaxy, a rotating wonder of bright lights, stars, and planets, but mostly, space. Our bodies, what we see and consider "solid," composed of atoms, electrons, rotating and subject to those same gravitational forces, and also, almost all space.

But beware your misguided senses! This is not emptiness. Just, for most of us, an unseen, unknown.

When I consider the fundamental questions in life—*How? Why?*—I feel a profound frustration so deep it almost hurts. I am limited, only see what I see, know what I can know.

My dogs, and the buzzing bees—even they know and see things that I cannot. We humans are profound and yet so very simple, and wrong, in our ways, in our understanding.

And yet, when I most need comfort—these observations comfort me. The sea crashing. The stars—holding the same elements that compose all that I can see around me, and in me.

I do not need to know how, and anyhow I cannot. Nor do I need to know why.

In the end, I am part of this larger composition, a cacophony of elements, mathematical and physical. My composition will change over time, a strand of melody against a larger symphony. In the end, all I can know with certainty, as the poet said, is that I am.

One day, I will return to the earth, decompose into other forms, perhaps nurture other life, or one day, as our planet ends, be distributed into the universe as part of the stuff—the elements of everything. It's strangely reassuring. Science as spirituality.

So, then, let me focus on the small pool of life I inhabit. Even as an adult living far from the sea, the ocean of life crashes noisily around me. Dangerous, exciting, reassuring. And in my small tide pool, I find the things where I dwell to be real, meaningful, contained. My life, the people I love.

I am, and allow myself to exist.

About the Authors

MerriLee Anderson is a clinical psychologist who is beginning to consider herself a writer. Her essays have recently appeared in *HerStry*, *You Might Need to Hear This*, and *bioStories*. She lives in Dallas, Texas with her wife, Jill, and mutts, Rosie and Daisy. She finds joy in connecting with people, be it through writing or conversation.

Susan P. Epstein is a writer and psychotherapist who draws on decades of clinical experience to explore the complexity of memory, loss, and human connection. Her work is rooted in deep listening—to her clients, her past, and the quiet moments that shape us. The author of a professional book on therapeutic techniques for working with youth, she now brings that same depth and insight to her creative nonfiction. Susan lives in New London, Connecticut.

Eileen Fitzmaurice is a former instructor of English as a Second Language and a magazine editor, with a love for language that has inspired her career path. She currently works at a large university in New York City, helping students find their passion. Writing has been a calling since the age of nine, when Eileen crafted *Encyclopedia Brown*-inspired mysteries on an old typewriter in her childhood kitchen. She is an empty-nester, obsessed with piecing together her spotty Irish heritage and excited for life's next adventure.

Ann Goethe is a pseudonym. Like most writers, Ann cannot silence the stories that start as tiny nuggets and, over time, beg to be released. It is her dream to one day give these stories her undivided attention, but until then, she writes whenever time allows. She lives in Michigan with her two dogs, loves cold weather, and is working on a romantasy novel. Ann was previously published in *Elegant Literature*; you can read more at www.anngoethewrites.com.

Lynne Golodner is the award-winning author of 12 bestselling books, a writing coach and retreat leader, and a marketing entrepreneur through her company, Your People LLC. She lives in metro Detroit and is the mother of four young adults. Lynne created and facilitates The Writers Community. Learn more at https://lynnegolodner.com.

Anita John lives in the Scottish Borders and writes theatre scripts, poetry and short fiction. She's a founding member of Borders Pub Theatre (bringing new theater writing to new audiences); a member of the poetry and piano trio *Contrappuntistica* (performing themed poetry and piano evenings throughout the Scottish Borders); and a creative writing tutor. Love and loss, nature, family and inter-generational relationships form the core of her work: https://anitajohn.co.uk

April Krassner is a writer living in Bridgeport, Connecticut. Her work has appeared in print and online in more than a dozen publications including *Poetry Breakfast, Anderbo,* and *Star82 Review.* When not writing, she is frequently thinking about sentences, and phrases. Sometimes she even drills down into words.

Liwen grew up in China and came to the United States in her 20s. She lives in New York City and writes for local publications there. Her piece included in this anthology was not previously published but was presented in a live show called "Generation Women" in Joe's Pub, a public theater in New York City in November 2024 (with minor changes).

Bonnie Jess Lopane enjoyed a career in nonprofit marketing and fundraising for 40 years, from which she retired in May 2025. She was Vice President, Chief Development Officer, for Hospice & Community Care, a program of Choices Healthcare, the largest nonprofit hospice provider in Pennsylvania. Writing has been a significant part of her work and, following the unexpected death of her husband in 2010, she found writing to be a meaningful part of her grief and healing process. Bonnie has always wanted to be a writer beyond her employment and is looking forward to creating a writing career in retirement.

Jane McCauley is a re-emerging writer after a hiatus to raise a family and explore the world. She has been a featured reader for the Walker Art Center Poetry Series and published in a collection of broadsides to commemorate the event. Aside from writing, Jane loves to hang with her husband and pup. She also enjoys packing up the car for a road trip, getting on an airplane to anywhere, and a brisk hike in the mountains.

Jessica Montague is a relationship therapist in private practice and co-founder of Relatable, an app that brings relational intelligence to the masses. She lives in the Bay Area with her husband, two children, and their Shih-Tzu, Charlie.

Alyssa Musso is a scientist by trade but a creative at heart. When she is not working full-time as a toxicologist, she enjoys writing fiction as well as some shorter creative nonfiction pieces. Alyssa is currently working on completing the first draft of her thriller/suspense novel, which has been a work-in-progress for many years. She plans to publish her first novel soon with hopes of publishing many more in the future.

Claire Newman is a writer and corgi lover who lives in Dallas, Texas with her husband, Phil. She is an Executive Producer on the upcoming documentary film, *Women Laughing*, about female cartoonists at *the New Yorker*, both past and present, and creating change through humor. Claire has two grown children.

Ciara O'Laoire is a writer and home cook. After living throughout the world she has settled in Huntington Woods, Michigan with her husband and two young children. Her food based chronicles can be found at @atableinthewoods on Instagram.

Meggie Orgain is a writer, sommelier, and mother of two from Texas. She earned a Bachelor of Arts in English from Southwestern University and a Juris Doctorate from Texas Tech University School of Law. She enjoys writing about the grittier, sometimes darker, sides of motherhood, and her flash fiction story *Make A Wish* received an Honorable Mention in Round 1 of the 2022 NYC Midnight 250-word Microfiction Challenge. She is currently working on her first novel in Dallas where she lives with her family.

Mandy Prell investigates the female body, sexuality, motherhood, marriage, and faith through a feminist lens. She holds an M.S.Ed. from Johns Hopkins University and currently works as an adjunct professor in Louisville, Kentucky where she lives with her daughters, spouse, and cats. Mandy writes with Lynne Golodner's international cohort The Writers Community, completed Lynne's Advanced Poets IndieMFA through WritingWorkshops.com and has participated in workshops from instructors Amanda Montei, Lynne Golodner, Joan Kwan Glass, Lauren Brazeal Garza, Mark Gottlieb, and Meg Eden. Her poetry has appeared in Gnashing Teeth Publishing zines and anthologies and on Paragraph Planet.

Carol Roehrig grew up in a rural Wisconsin community which formed her zeal for simple living. Once a successful entrepreneur, Carol turned her focus to stories around her, and now crafts essays and short fiction. She enjoys the outdoors, reading, knitting, and weaving words on the page. You can find her gazing at nature, hovering over words, and delighting in the ordinary. She resides in Dallas, Texas and Crested Butte, Colorado with her husband Fred.

Kate Rosenblum is a clinical psychologist and professor, and has published 200+ academic journal articles and op-ed pieces on topics related to her academic areas of expertise. Yet while she has always been an avid reader, and studied creative writing as an undergraduate many decades ago, it somehow took a breast cancer diagnosis in 2021 to give Kate the necessary nudge to return to writing. Her creative writing is predominantly memoir, with a frequent focus on short pieces that weave together reflections on illness, healing, and family relationships with observations and reflections on nature. She is working on a memoir of her cancer journey. Prior creative works have been published by breastcancer.org and in the poetry and medicine section of the *Journal of the American Medical Association*.

Maureen Shea grew up in Latin America, moving to New Orleans as an adult, where she accepted a position as a professor of Latin American Literature at Tulane University. She taught there for 35 years until her retirement in 2022. Now, she spends her time reading, writing, enjoying the New Orleans music scene, and delighting in walking the green spaces with her two German Shepherds.

Julie Song's parents left South Korea in the early 1970's and immigrated to Brooklyn, where she was born. The bitter winters were a bit too cold for them, so they packed her and her older sister into their Oldsmobile sedan and chased warmer weather in Southern California. Julie did her undergraduate education at the University of California, Irvine, where she majored in sociology. She continued her post-graduate education there, focusing on immigration, gender, and religion. Her research centered on the ways that Korean immigrants utilize religion to assimilate into the American mainstream. Julie completed a PhD and was hired as a professor in 2008. She is currently a tenured faculty member and the director of the Honors Program at her college. Her publications include *Exploring Society,* and several creative nonfiction essays. She is currently working on a novel about a young Korean American woman who is in an interracial relationship, navigating privilege, sexuality, and race.

Deena Staples is a wife to one husband, and the mother to three amazing children. She lives on a small island off the coast of Maine where she teaches second grade.

Barb Summers is a writer who grew up in rural Ontario, Canada, and now lives in a small town with her husband, son and their affectionate cat. She studied creative writing at the University of Toronto. She's had short fiction published in *Literary Mama* and nonfiction published on Mediu m.com. She's currently working on a debut novel of women's fiction. Barb works as a writer and editor for a community newspaper.

www.ingramcontent.com/pod-product-compliance
Lightning Source LLC
Chambersburg PA
CBHW031052310726
48969CB00007B/2237